A FORGOTTEN TRUTH

Other publications by D. M. A. Leggett
THE SACRED QUEST
WAR GAMES THAT SUPERPOWERS PLAY
(Booklet with C. M. Waterlow)

A FORGOTTEN TRUTH

A SPIRITUAL VISION FOR MODERN MAN

D. M. A. LEGGETT
M.A. (Cantab), D.Sc. (Lond)
F.R.Ae.S., F.I.M.A., F.K.C.

and

M. G. PAYNE
M.A., B.Sc. (Manchester)

PILGRIMS BOOK SERVICES
TASBURGH NORWICH ENGLAND

British Library Cataloguing in Publication Data

Leggett, D. M. A.
  A forgotten truth: a spiritual vision for modern man.
  1. Reincarnation
  I. Title   II. Payne, M. G.
  291.2′37   BL515

ISBN 0–946259–14–3

Photoset by Waveney Typesetters, Norwich
and printed by The Thetford Press Ltd.,
Thetford, Norfolk

Prologue

If and when the imaginative vision of the spiritual man and the research of the psychologist into the conditioning of the human soul combine, man's understanding of himself and of his essential vocation in life will be immeasurably deepened. He will begin then to exercise his reason aright, realising that to open the mind need not mean to close the heart, but to cleanse and clarify it, and that only in the reason of a purified heart can the mind be truly enlightened. Then, indeed, man's feet will be once again on 'the Way' from which he has wandered throughout his history so often and so disastrously, but to which every great teacher has sought to recall him.

Hugh L'Anson Faussett, *The Last Dimension*, 1966

It is no longer possible to believe that any political or economic reform, or scientific advance, or technological progress could solve the life-and-death problems of industrial society. They lie too deep, in the heart and soul of every one of us. It is there that the main work of reform has to be done – secretly, unobtrusively.

The most basic need of our time is the need for metaphysical reconstruction, a supreme effort to bring clarity into our deepest convictions with regard to the questions – What is man? Where does he come from? What is the purpose of his life?

E. F. Schumacher, *Good Work*, 1979

Contents

Preface

In certain respects *A Forgotten Truth* is a sequel to *The Sacred Quest*. The latter was mainly concerned with the question 'What is the purpose of human life on this planet?' Evidence was reviewed and some provisional conclusions reached. In the process there emerged a strong case for serial existence – reincarnation in its little understood form. In the present book the 'forgotten truth' is reincarnation, and its subject matter is the far reaching implications of this difficult but very important concept.

D.M.A.L. is responsible for the contents of Chapters 1 to 6. For Chapters 7 to 10 responsibility is shared equally between D.M.A.L. and M.G.P.

The authors are deeply grateful to Sir Kelvin Spencer for many constructive comments and suggestions and for contributing a Foreword, and to Mrs W. D. Woods for typing the final manuscript.

Foreword

So far as we know, Man is the only species that is deliberately creating conditions which could bring about his own extinction. The fossil record shows that life has taken many forms during the thousands of millions of years of its evolving manifestations on this planet. Many of these forms have flourished for a while and then become extinct. It seems as though a life force is experimenting with types of expression appropriate to the conditions here and has made many false starts. Could mankind be yet another?

This book gives a provisional answer. That answer is *YES – unless he wakes up in time to change course*. What appears to be a unique feature in the cause of his potential demise is that it is self-created. The evolution of his intelligence seems to have run far ahead of his growth in wisdom. Intellect unguided by wisdom spells disaster. It has spawned technologies that enable man to make drastic changes to the environment, to the crust of the earth, the vegetation, rivers, sea and air. And changes to the chemical content of the upper atmosphere, which at present shields us from cosmic radiation harmful to life, is a threatening and imminent possibility. The justification for this statement is summarised in the last chapter of this book – 'Summary and Conclusions'.

A Forgotten Truth is a challenging and well-referenced account of the many causes that point to this gloomy prophesy. But it is not just one more depressing treatise on the ills of the world today. Far from it. The authors give sound reasons for hope that we can navigate safely through the rocks ahead if, but only if, we change course in time. And for that change to come about we must remind the decision-makers, who shape our lives, of a forgotten truth. That truth is summed up by the authors as 'a "framework of faith", . . . a vision that will give purpose and meaning to human life.' From the dawn of history until some three centuries ago western man had such a faith, expressed in religious terms. But that faith has become obscured in dogmas which, relevant at the time they

xi

were formed, no longer convey the meaning they did. Many of us are put off by parts of the dogmas which blur the deep truths they initially conveyed to communities with world views very different from those now current. Sir Alister Hardy, FRS, in his 1964 Gifford Lectures published as *The Divine Flame*, expresses it thus:

> Our civilization has been built upon a spiritual interpretation of the world; if the majority of the population come to have a materialistic outlook the whole nature of our way of life may change, and not I think for the better.

In the more than eight decades of my life I have been saddened and alarmed as I have watched Sir Alister's prophesy becoming all too apparent.

But there is not justification for despair. In the darkest days of the 1939–45 war, Winston Churchill gave the nation a clarion call:

> Let us therefore brace ourselves to our duties, and so bear ourselves that, if the British Empire and its Commonwealth last for a thousand years, men will still say, '*This* was their finest hour.'

The authors of *A Forgotten Truth* make a comparable call for action to a far greater danger than faced us in that war. Their call is not expressed with the oratorical splendour of a Churchill, nor should it be. Both authors have won eminence in the academic world and follow the tradition of writing with calm deliberation based on accurate up-to-date knowledge. They paint the picture with clarity and force. Their conclusions are soundly based: mankind must wake up to the forgotten truth that he is a spiritual being, and spirit can move mountains.

Let us then take their message to heart, study the book and the references, and each of us take what action he can to see that mankind changes course in time.

> Nobody made a greater mistake than he who did nothing because he could only do a little. Edmund Burke

Sir Kelvin Spencer, M.C., C.B.E.

Acknowledgements

The authors wish to thank the following persons and publishers for permission to quote from their books:

Robinson Books Ltd, for quotations from *Bhagavad Gita, translated with an introduction and commentary* by Charles Johnston, published by John M. Watkins (1965); and for quotations from *The Yoga Sutras of Patanjali, an interpretation* by Charles Johnston, published by J. M. Watkins (1949).

Hutchinson Books Ltd, for quotations from *The Occult Way* by P. G. Bowen, published by The Occult Book Society (1938); and for quotations from *The Sayings of the Ancient One* by P. G. Bowen, published by Rider & Co. (1935).

Oxford University Press, for quotations from *Some Sayings of the Buddha, according to the Pali Canon*, translated by F. L. Woodward.

Hodder & Stoughton Ltd, for quotations from *The Romeo Error* by Lyall Watson.

Wildwood House Ltd, for permission to quote excerpts from *The Tao of Physics* by Fritjof Capra (1975).

Thorsons Publishing Group, for quotations from *The Medium, the Mystic, and the Physicist* by Lawrence LeShan, published by Turnstone Press (1974).

George Allen & Unwin, for quotations from *Living On* by Paul Beard.

Sun Publishing Co., Albuquerque, U.S.A., for quotations from *Rolling Thunder* by J. R. Jochmans.

H. K. Challoner for quotations from *The Wheel of Rebirth*, published by Rider & Co. (1935).

The C. W. Daniel Company Ltd, for quotation from *A Man Seen Afar* by W. Tudor Pole & Rosamond Lehmann, published by Neville Spearman Ltd (1965).

The Theosophical Publishing House Ltd, for quotations from *Man Incarnate* by P. D. Bendit & Laurence Bendit.

Faber & Faber Ltd, for quotations from *The Psychic Sense*, by P. D. Payne & L. J. Bendit.

Lucis Thrust, New York, for quotations from *A Treatise on White Magic* by Alice A. Bailey, published by Lucis Publishing Co. (1934).

The Editor of the *Burrswood Herald*, for permission to quote from an article by Peter Spink.

The authors also wish to thank Roger Evans, Director of the Institute for Psychosynthesis, London, for advice about quotations from *Psychosynthesis* by Roberto Assagioli, published by Hobbs, Dorman & Co. Inc. New York (1965).

Forbearance is asked for if the authors have overlooked, or failed to trace, any source from which permission to quote ought to have been sought.

Part I

1: What Constitutes Evidence?

What is ordinarily referred to as evidence is of many different kinds. There are, for example, the measurements and readings on which scientists base their hypotheses; or what the observers of an accident say they saw or heard; or the descriptions by mystics of what they claim to have experienced. These three examples illustrate the great range of what is commonly referred to as evidence and, for convenience, will be referred to as evidence of types (a), (b) and (c).

In (a) the measurements and readings are numerical, and there is little scope for error in recording them. The validity of the actual experiment is provided by its *repeatability*, and the fact that *tests conducted under similar conditions give similar results*.

In (b) the use of words presents no problem, but experience shows surprising scope for error in reporting what actually took place. This is shown by an experiment conducted by a professor of law during a lecture on evidence. Unbeknown to the members of his class, the professor had arranged that during his lecture three people should dash into the lecture room; that one of the three, when in front of the class, should fire three blanks from a revolver in quick succession; and that the three intruders should then dash out – with the class encouraged to give chase! The accounts by the students of what they thought had taken place often differed significantly from what had actually happened.[1] As the exact reconstruction of an accident is rarely possible, deciding what occurred depends on the overall *consistency* of the observers' accounts.

1

In (c) the experience transcends what is capable of being described in numbers or words, and so in a literal sense is 'indescribable'. Moreover, the experience is unique to the individual concerned, so that no direct check is possible on what is being claimed. If, however, the accounts of such experiences, when undergone by different people on different occasions, display certain similarities, then the presence of these similarities may have important evidential value.

Generalising: evidence of type (a) is objective; evidence of type (c) is subjective; evidence of type (b) is a combination of the two.

Today's psychological climate is largely the result of the successes achieved by science during the last 150 years: successes arising from the use of objective data and experiments that are repeatable. But because of these successes, what tends to be overlooked is a realisation of how much of our lives lies outside what science is equipped to investigate. An actual situation almost always involves a subjective element, and events which are exactly repeatable are very rare. Reflection leads to the conclusion that while objective data derived from repeatable experiments can lead to proof and certainty, life as lived is not like this. In practice, certainty is replaced by varying degrees of probability. The probability that the alarm will go off, that we shall wake up feeling well, that the postman will call, that the car will start, that the train will run, etc., etc. What matters, for normal living, is the degree of probability that these events will happen. And how is this arrived at? Answer – 'By noting what has happened in the past; by *the cumulative evidence of past experience.*' And for most of the time there is little more to be said. But what are we to make of an unusual experience which appears to contravene scientific laws as at present formulated? Such as an apparent case of telepathy or precognition, or an intimation from someone who has died? Such experiences will be referred to as paranormal and have occasioned much interest, difficulty and controversy.

The interest lies partly in the actual happenings, e.g. in the information about a particular individual that may be received by ostensibly paranormal means, and partly in the scientific and philosophic implications of such happenings. To explore the unknown is one thing, and usually welcomed; but to come up with observations and conclusions which run counter to current thinking is another and not infrequently viewed with misgiving. To the latter category belongs the paranormal, because much of what happens or is experienced does not fit into the dominant current outlook of scientific humanism, the view that there is nothing outside the world of the five physical senses and which asserts that, given time, everything will be explicable in terms of physics and chemistry.

Now comes the difficulty. Having regard to the tenacity with which scientific humanism is held in many quarters, the evidence – if it is to be taken seriously – for anything which opposes it has to be very strong. Repeatable and repeated experiments under controlled conditions say the scientists. But these are just the conditions which the student of the paranormal can rarely provide. For more often than not the paranormal is not susceptible to that kind of investigation. As a result the scientific community has tended, albeit with notable exceptions, to give the whole subject the cold shoulder and to ignore it. But the topic has not gone away. Since the end of World War II, there has been a marked upsurge of interest in many aspects of the paranormal, and a small number of devoted researchers have produced results of definite scientific interest. This has led to controversy. On one side are those who take the *a priori* view that there *cannot* be anything beyond or outside the world of the five physical senses, and that therefore those who maintain that there is are mistaken. Such people point out – not without some justification – that in the past the whole subject has been shot through with deliberate fraud or unconscious deception, and that therefore whatever is being asserted today has little or no credibility. On the other side are the devoted research groups – very few in the U.K., many more in the U.S.A. – who have been collecting and sifting data and, where possible, experimenting. These groups are totally convinced that the paranormal is a vast area about which we know very little, is worthy of serious investigation, and may prove to be most important. In between are the great majority, both of the general public and of the scientific community, who view the subject, in so far as they view it at all, with an odd mixture of curiosity and unease.

Much of the difficulty impeding progress is due to the impossibility of obtaining objective data from repeated experiments; what was referred to at the beginning of this chapter as evidence type (a). But, as has already been pointed out, this is not the only kind of evidence on which we base our lives, or, indeed, on which the law of the land is founded. Most of the offenders who are sentenced in a court of law for committing a crime, including those which until recently carried the death penalty, are convicted on evidence type (b) – evidence which is a mixture of the objective and subjective, but the overall consistency of which led to a conclusion which was 'beyond reasonable doubt'.

Has this approach to evidence got any application to a study of the paranormal? An unprejudiced answer must surely be that it has. Instead of insisting that the only acceptable data are the results of repeatable experiments under controlled conditions, suppose we take as data *the cumulative evidence of reliably recorded happenings*. Such evidence exists in plenty in certain well defined areas of paranormal experience (see Chapter 5), and in certain of these areas it may be possible to formulate working hypotheses (not to be confused with established theories). What seems strange is the widespread reluctance to do just this. For example, when some experience or happening *indicates* the possibility or probability of survival as the simplest explanatory hypothesis, the reaction so often seems to be: 'We cannot stand for that (i.e. survival). So we shall have to think of some other explanation.' It is almost as if survival was regarded as the ultimate calamity! Is this, I wonder, because scientific humanism and the attendant belief that nothing exists outside the world of the five physical senses has entered so deeply into the conscious and subconscious minds of the average person that he or she has come to regard the concept of survival as something to be eschewed?

Reference

1. Referred to by Alistair Cooke in one of his *Letters from America*

2: The Distinctive Roles of Science and Religion

In the West, relations between science and religion have tended to be uneasy, periods of relatively peaceful coexistence being punctuated by periods of acute tension. Two such times which immediately spring to mind are those associated with Galileo in the early sixteen hundreds and with Charles Darwin half way through last century. The former asserted that the earth went round the sun, and not vice versa; the latter that plants and animals had evolved by a process of natural selection (i.e. by survival of the fittest), and that man, at least so far as his body was concerned, had evolved from the animals. When these discoveries were first proclaimed, the attitude of the Church was hostile and led to conflict. In order to probe the cause of these conflicts and whether they were justified, it is necessary to define *science* and *religion*.

Science is defined in the *Oxford Dictionary* as 'systematised knowledge', that is, knowledge which can be measured or classified. Religion is less easy to define, but in *Chambers Encyclopedia* is referred to as 'the word generally used to describe man's relation to divine or superhuman powers and the various organised systems of belief and worship in which these relations have been expressed'. Put a little differently, religion is the life of the spirit; the intuitive recognition by man that he possesses a spiritual nature, and the extent to which he manifests that nature. In neither of these two definitions is religion either measurable or classifiable.

Science is concerned with quantity; religion with quality. Science is primarily interested in the form; religion with the consciousness which animates the form. Science is essentially objective, religion is largely subjective. In a way, the roles of science and religion correspond to the outline and colour in a painting. The outline provides the framework, the colour portrays the spirit.

With science and religion so defined, it follows that their respective roles are *complementary* and, though contiguous, rarely, if ever, overlap. How is it then that from time to time tension and conflict have occurred? The answer is: 'When either science or religion have stepped outside their rightful domain and made claims to which they were not entitled.' In the case of Galileo, whether the earth went round the sun or vice versa, had nothing to do with religion as properly defined and understood. But the ecclesiastical authorities at that time thought that it had; hence the controversy. With regard to Darwin, the situation was more difficult since evolution is a subject which is of concern to both science and religion, but viewed from different standpoints. Science is primarily concerned with *how* evolution has taken place, that is, with the mechanisms by which some species of plant or animal has given rise to another species, often of greater complexity, and ultimately to man. But *why* evolution has occurred, why in the sense of to what goal or for what purpose, is a religious question with which science has little or no concern. The Scottish Catechism, for example, states that 'Man's chief end is to glorify God and to enjoy him for ever', an essentially religious statement on which science is not qualified to comment.

The answer to *how* evolution has occurred depends on measurement and classification and is therefore an eminently appropriate field for scientific investigation. The answer to *why, for what purpose*, is not something which can be measured or classified, but depends on values. And these are the province of religion. Why then did Darwin's theory of evolution produce such a violent and, from the Church, hostile reaction? From accounts written at the time, it would seem due to the belief, implicit rather than explicit, that consciousness was a product of matter, physical matter – the view on which scientific humanism is based – and that because evolution of the physical form of plants and animals and finally man had been 'adequately' explained by the process of natural selection, so had the evolution of consciousness. Consciousness had evolved as the form had evolved – automatically. There was no place for the concept of special creation, and therefore no need to postulate the existence of God.

Whether 'adequately' is an appropriate word to describe the current view or views of evolution is open to question. That natural selection has been a major factor in bringing about evolution there can be no doubt. But 'gaps' persist. How explain, for example, the gradual development of an eye? A progressively sensitive area which could not, on the face of it, bestow any advantage on its possessor until it had become an, at least partially, effective organ of vision?[1]

Previously, it was suggested that conflict between science and religion occurred when either science or religion stepped outside their rightful domain and made claims to which they were not entitled. Let us now see how this applies to the conflict over evolution. Stripped of inessentials the controversy arose from two incompatible views about the nature of man. The view of many Darwinians, though not necessarily of Darwin himself, was that man consisted of his physical body and of that only, and that to suggest the existence of soul or spirit independent of the physical body was illusory. The orthodox Christian view was that man's being was at least twofold – body and soul – and perhaps threefold – body, soul, and spirit.[2] In this conflict both parties were at fault. The scientists, qua scientists, were quite unjustified in expressing an opinion about the existence of the soul and spirit of man, and of how this had evolved or come into existence. The Church party, on the other hand, was equally unjustified in asserting what could, or could not, be true regarding the evolution of man's physical body. Both parties to the dispute had stepped outside their rightful domain and had made claims to which they were not entitled.

An apt commentary on the attitudes responsible for such conflicts is provided by the following extract from a paper presented by Willis Harman at a Conference on *Science et Conscience* at Cordoba in October 1979.

> Scientists of an earlier generation were guilty of overclaiming when, with abundant hubris, they dismissed religion as pre-scientific theories about matters on which scientists would eventually have a later word, if not the last. To be sure, the religionists were particularly vulnerable when they insisted that characteristics of the physical world – such as relative positions of earth and sun, the age of the earth, and the physical ancestors of humankind – should be established by Holy Writ rather than empirical observation. But the scientists, on the other hand, were egregiously arrogant in insisting that all the religions of the world were based in illusion since the realm of human experience they took as central was not caught in the net cast by science.

A major factor in the tremendous successes achieved by science during the last 150 years has been the use of the scientific method. This is the name given to the three-fold process of collecting data relevant to the particular problem being investigated; framing a hypothesis (i.e. making a guess) as to what will explain the data; and then testing the hypothesis by appropriate experiments. As an example, let us see how Newton's Law of Gravitation was derived. Stage one was the observed fact that when any body, small or large, light or heavy, was raised from the earth's surface and released, it fell to the ground. The problem – Why? What was it that prompted bodies to fall? Stage two consisted of putting forward the hypothesis that *any* two bodies are attracted to each other by a force which is directly proportional to the product of their masses and inversely proportional to the square of the distance between them. Stage three consisted of testing this hypothesis by obser-vation or experiment. An especially significant test was provided by observing the orbits in which the planets revolved around the sun. Were these orbits, which were observed to be elliptical, consistent with Newton's Law of Gravitation? The answer, of course, is 'Yes, they were'. But at the time, three and a half centuries ago, this discovery which we now take for granted, marked a great step forward in understanding the motion of the heavenly bodies. An important characteristic of a scientific hypothesis is that though it may be proved false, usually as a result of some experiment, it can never be proved true. All that can be affirmed is that a particular hypothesis is consistent with certain experimental results. In practice, most working hypotheses are only valid, i.e. supported by experiment, over a particular range of the variables involved and to a certain degree of accuracy. If the accuracy is great and the tests are numerous, the hypothesis is sometimes referred to as a law, e.g. Newton's Law of Gravitation. But most hypotheses are not like that, and changes may be rapid. For this reason scientific hypotheses are sometimes referred to as models. Consider, for instance, the concept of matter. A century ago matter was thought to consist of exceedingly small indivisible particles. Fifty years later each particle had become a kind of miniature solar system. And now? The solar system model has been shown to be inadequate and been replaced by . . .? Difficult to say! In a period of just over one hundred years there have been three different models. It is, however, important to appreciate that an outdated model may still be useful. In the case of matter, for example, each of the outdated models has wide ranging use and application.

Having noted the vital part played by the scientific method in the development of science, it is natural to enquire whether anything comparable exists in the religious field. The suggestion is now made that there is. If the problem posed is: Who or what is God? What is the purpose of human life?, let us see what might correspond to the three stages of the scientific method when applied to this particular problem. Stage one is collecting relevant data, and we must consider what comes under this heading. Reflection suggests that relevant data are the *fons et origo* of the great religious traditions; and, of these, attention has been focussed on Hinduism, the Hermetic Tradition,[3] Buddhism and Christianity. In the case of Buddhism and Christianity the foundation is the life and sayings of Gautama the Buddha and of Jesus the Christ. In Hinduism and the Hermetic Tradition the situation is more difficult as there is nothing which corresponds to the life and sayings of an original founder. Instead, we have chosen certain texts from Hindu and Hermetic literature which are deemed by their followers to be of fundamental importance. In each of these religious traditions there are today many sects and schools of thought. But whatever the sect or school of thought, there are very few who would not accept the relevance and importance of the passages quoted from within their own tradition. The disagreements which have led to sect or schism arise, not from whether what is recorded was actually said, but from differences of emphasis and interpretation of what was said. For it must always be borne in mind that the world's scriptures are concerned with the life of the spirit, to describe which words are not entirely satisfactory, though they are all we have. Our everyday lives are mainly taken up with thinking, feeling and doing, and for such functions words are well adapted. But the life of the spirit involves something more, and when referring to this words have to be regarded as symbols and interpreted accordingly. It is not just chance that the great religious teachers have all made such extensive use of metaphor, allegory, and parable. To describe the transcendent they could scarcely do otherwise.

Now what corresponds to the second stage of the scientific method, that of framing a hypothesis, i.e. making a guess as to what will explain the data – the inspired writings in the case of Hinduism and the Hermetic Tradition, and the reported sayings of Gautama and Jesus in the case of Buddhism and Christianity? The answer is the dogmatic statements of belief which have been formulated and declared official by the relevant ecclesiastical authority. This

11

prompts three observations. First, Gautama and Jesus never propounded dogmatic statements of belief. Indeed, the former is reputed to have said: 'Never accept anything that I, the Buddha (which means the enlightened one) say, unless it appeals to your reason.' These formulated statements were made by the *followers* of Gautama and Jesus, never by the teachers themselves. Second, these dogmatic statements were inevitably coloured by the knowledge and outlook current at the time they were formulated. As the centuries pass, knowledge and outlook change – during the last century and a half with great rapidity – but in the case of Christianity the dogmatic statements have remained, to all intents and purposes, unaltered. Third, until quite recently Christians had little knowledge of what Hindus and Buddhists thought and believed, and vice versa. And the same is true of the Hermetic teaching.

Which brings us to the third stage of the scientific method: testing the hypothesis by observation and experiment. What corresponds to this? The answer, surely, is *experience*. For example, the individual experience of the mystic; the repeatable experiments of science; and the cumulative evidence of the paranormal. In Galileo's time this third stage was ignored, with disastrous results for the Christian Church. Asked in all humility, is there not a danger today of the Church repeating its mistake – this time in relation to the paranormal – by not taking sufficient note of the considerable and increasing body of evidence regarding the higher psychism, the nature of life after death, and the possibility of serial existence and its far reaching implications?

The next three chapters are devoted to the application of the scientific method to the problem posed by the three fundamental questions: Who or what is God? Who or what is man? What is the purpose of human life? Chapter 3 assembles the data or, more precisely, a sample of the data – evidence from some of the world's scriptures. Chapter 4 appraises this evidence, preparatory to framing a working hypothesis which is consistent with it. Chapter 5 considers how the formulated hypothesis stands up to mystical experience, now recognised as being far more widespread than had previously been thought; to recent developments in biology, physics, and psychology; and to evidence from the paranormal.

References

1. See, for example, a review article by John Davy – 'Once upon a time' – published in *The Observer Review* of August 16th, 1981
2. At the eighth Ecumenical Council in 869, the Church affirmed the dual nature of man – body and soul – which accordingly replaced the Pauline tripartite division of body, soul, and spirit
3. The religion of ancient Egypt.

3: Evidence from the Scriptures

In this chapter we shall consider the data, preparatory to formulating a working hypothesis.

The four sources referred to in the previous chapter differ greatly in style and approach, and reflect the culture and characteristics of the people amongst whom the teaching originated (Hinduism and the Hermetic Tradition) or to whom it was addressed (Buddhism and Christianity). For each source, consideration is given to teachings about God, fundamental principles, and application, and ends with a prayer or parable.

Hinduism

The passages from Hinduism have been largely drawn from the *Bhagavad Gita* and the *Yoga Sutras of Patanjali*. The dates of these two texts are not known, but they were probably compiled over a considerable period of time. Both were in existence by the beginning of the Christian era.

About the *Gita*, Charles Johnston writes as follows:

> There is but one problem of life; throughout all lands, in all ages, it has been the same. It is the problem of the soul and immortality. From difference of temperament or race, or both, there have been certain widely divergent lines in the effort of ancient India to solve the immemorial secret. Each had its growth and development; each its long line of adherents; each its controversies, its commentators, its triumphs. In course of time the difference between these systems grew more marked than their agreement, and controversy overshadowed appreciation. One great task of the *Bhagavad Gita* is that of reconciler

14

between these divergent systems, and the revelation of the truth that they all lead to a single goal.[1]

About the *Yoga Sutras of Patanjali*, Charles Johnston writes:

> The theme is the great regeneration, the birth of the spiritual from the psychical man.
>
> We think of ourselves as living a purely physical life, in these material bodies of ours. In reality, we have gone far indeed from pure physical life; for ages, our life has been psychical, we have been centred and immersed in the psychic nature. The teaching of the East is that the psychical man is the veil and prophecy of the spiritual man. The purpose of life, therefore, is the realising of that prophecy; the unveiling of the immortal man; the birth of the spiritual from that psychical, whereby we enter our divine inheritance and come to inhabit Eternity.
>
> Patanjali has in mind the spiritual man, to be born from the psychical. His purpose is to set in order the practical means for the unveiling and regeneration, and to indicate the fruit, the glory and the power, of that new birth.[2]

The quotations from the *Gita* are from the translation by Charles Johnston; the quotations from the *Aphorisms of Patanjali* are from the translation contained in *The Light of the Soul – the Yoga Sutras of Patanjali* by Alice Bailey.[3]

About God

> Though I am the Unborn, the Soul that passes not away, though I am the lord of beings, yet as lord over My nature I become manifest, through the magical power of the Soul.
>
> For whenever there is a withering of the Law, and an uprising of lawlessness on all sides, then I manifest Myself.
>
> For the salvation of the righteous, and the destruction of such as do evil; for the firm establishing of the Law I come to birth in age after age.
>
> *Bhagavad Gita* [B.G.] Bk 4:6–8

> I know all beings, the past, the present, those that are to come; but Me none knows.
>
> B.G. Bk 7:26

All manifest things spring forth from the Unmanifest, at the coming of the Day; and at the coming of the Night, they melt away into the Unmanifest again.

The whole host of beings, coming into being again and again, melts away at the coming of the Night, and comes forth inevitably at the coming of the Day.

But beyond this manifest Being, there is another Being, unmanifest, everlasting, which does not pass away, even when all beings perish.

That Unmanifest is called the Everlasting, and this they call the Supreme Way, gaining which they return not again; this is My highest home.

This supreme Spirit is to be found by undivided love; in This all beings dwell, by This was the universe stretched forth.

B.G. Bk 8:18–22

For I am the resting place of the Eternal, of unfading immortality, of immemorial law and perfect joy.

B.G. Bk 14:27

Fundamental Principles

Tat twam asi – THAT art thou.

The Atman, the Self, is never born and never dies. It is without a cause and is eternally changeless. It is beyond time, unborn, permanent and everlasting.

Katha Upanishad

The beginnings of things are unmanifest, their mid course is manifest; their ending is unmanifest; what cause is here for lamentation?'

B.G. Bk 2:28

Let him not exult when he meets happiness, let him not grieve when he meets sorrow; firm in soul-vision, undeluded, knowing the Eternal, he stands firm in the Eternal.

When with soul detached from contact of outer things, he finds all happiness in the Soul, joined in union with the Eternal, he reaches everlasting joy.

For delights born of contact with outer things are wombs of pain; they have their beginning and their ending; in them the wise finds no delight.

16

He who even here, before the liberation from the body, is able to withstand the impetuous rush of desire and wrath, he is united, he is the happy man.

Who finds his Joy within, his paradise within, his light within, that master of union, becomes the Eternal, wins Nirvana, union with the Eternal.

The seers win Nirvana, union with the Eternal, whose sins are worn away, who have cut the knot of separateness, who are self-mastered, who delight in the weal of all beings.

Nirvana, union with the Eternal, has come nigh to those who are rid of desire and wrath, who have gained control, who control their thoughts, who have beheld the Soul.

B.G. Bk 5:19–25

The following instruction concerneth the Science of Union.

This Union (or Yoga) is achieved through the subjugation of the psychic nature, and the restraint of the chitta (or mind).

When this has been accomplished, the Yogi knows himself as he is in reality.

Up till now the inner man has identified himself with his forms and with their active modifications.

The control of these modifications of the internal organ, the mind, is to be brought about through tireless endeavour and through non-attachment.

Tireless endeavour is the constant effort to restrain the modifications of the mind.

When the object to be gained is sufficiently valued, and the efforts towards its attainment are persistently followed without intermission, then the steadiness of the mind is secured.

Non-attachment is freedom from longing for all objects of desire, either earthly or traditional, either here or hereafter.

The attainment of this state (spiritual consciousness) is rapid for those whose will is intensely alive.

Aphorisms of Patanjali [A.P.] Bk 1:1–4, 12–15, 21

The Yoga of action, leading to union with the soul is fiery aspiration, spiritual reading and devotion to Ishvara [God as a personal Being].

The aim of these three is to bring about soul vision and to eliminate obstructions.

These are the difficulty producing hindrances: avidya

17

[ignorance], the sense of personality, desire, hate and the sense of attachment.

Avidya is the cause of all the other obstructions whether they be latent, in process of elimination, overcome, or in full operation.

Avidya is the condition of confusing the permanent, pure, blissful and the Self with that which is impermanent, impure, painful and the not-self.

The sense of personality is due to the identification of the knower with the instruments of knowledge.

Intense desire for sentient existence is attachment. This is inherent in every form, is self-perpetuating, and known even to the very wise.

These five hindrances, when subtly known, can be overcome by an opposing mental attitude.

Karma itself has its root in these five hindrances and must come to fruition in this life or in some later life.

So long as the roots [or samskaras] exist, their fruition will be birth, life, and the experiences resulting in pleasure or pain.

These seeds [or samskaras] produce pleasure or pain according as their originating cause was good or evil.

All that is exists for the sake of the soul.

When the means to yoga have been steadily practised, and when impurity has been overcome, enlightenment takes place, leading up to full illumination.

A.P. Bk 2:1–6, 9–14, 21, 28

When concentration, meditation and contemplation form one sequential act, then is sanyama achieved.

As a result of sanyama comes the shining forth of the light.

This illumination is gradual; it is developed stage by stage.

Through the cultivation of this habit of mind there will eventuate a steadiness of spiritual perception.

The establishing of this habit, and the restraining of the mind from its thought-form-making tendency, results eventually in the constant power to contemplate.

Knowledge of previous incarnations becomes available when the power to see thought-images is acquired.

Those who have attained self-mastery can be seen and contacted through focussing the light in the head. This power is developed in one-pointed meditation.

18

All things can be known in the vivid light of the intuition.

A.P. Bk 3: 1–6, 10, 11, 18, 32, 33

The transfer of the consciousness from a lower vehicle into a higher is part of the great creative and evolutionary process.

The man who develops non-attachment even in his aspiration after illumination and isolated unity, becomes aware, eventually through practised discrimination, of the overshadowing cloud of spiritual knowledge.

When this stage is reached then the hindrances and karma are overcome.

When, through the removal of the hindrances and the purification of all the sheaths, the totality of knowledge becomes available, naught further remains for the man to do.

Time which is the sequence of the modifications of the mind, likewise terminates, giving place to the Eternal Now.

A.P. Bk 4:2, 29, 30, 31, 33

Application

Thy right is to the work, but never to its fruits; let not the fruit of thy work be thy motive, nor take refuge in abstinence from works.

B.G. Bk 2:47

Better one's own duty without excellence than the duty of another well followed out. Death in one's own duty is better; the duty of another is full of danger.

B.G. Bk 3:35

ARJUNA: This union through Oneness which is taught by Thee, – I perceive not its firm foundation, owing to the wavering of the mind. For the mind wavers, turbulent, impetuous, forceful; and I think it is as hard to hold as the wind!

THE MASTER: Without doubt, the wavering mind is hard to hold; but through assiduous practice, and through detachment it may be held firm.

B.G. Bk 6:33–35

Putting away hate for any being, friendly, pitiful, without desire or possessions, without vanity, equal in weal and woe, patient.

Content, ever following union, self-ruled, firmly determined,

19

with heart and soul centred in Me, who thus loves Me is beloved of Me.

He whom the world fears not, who fears not the world, free from exultation, anguish, fear, disquiet, such a one is beloved of Me.

Unconcerned, pure, direct, impartial, unperturbed, renouncing all personal initiatives, who thus loves Me is beloved of Me.

Who exults not nor hates nor grieves nor longs, renouncing fortune and misfortune, who is thus full of love is beloved of Me.

Equal to foe and friend, equal in honour, and dishonour, equal in cold and heat, weal and woe, from attachment altogether free.

Balanced in blame or praise, full of silence, content with whatever may befall, seeking no home here, steadfast-minded full of love, this man is beloved of Me.

And they who draw near to the righteous Immortal thus declared, full of faith, resting in Me, full of love, they are beyond all beloved of Me.

B.G. Bk 12:13–20

In the presence of him who has perfected harmlessness, all enmity ceases.

When truth to all beings is perfected, the effectiveness of his words and acts is immediately to be seen.

When abstention from theft is perfected, the yogi can have whatever he desires.

By abstention from incontinence, energy is acquired.

When abstention from avarice is perfected, there comes an understanding of the law of rebirth.

A.P. Bk 2:35–39

A Prayer

> O though who givest sustenance to the Universe
> From who all things proceed
> To whom all things return,
> Unveil to us the face of the true Spiritual Sun
> Hidden by a disc of golden light
> That we may know the Truth
> And do our whole duty
> As we journey to Thy Sacred Feet.

The Gayatri in the Rig-Veda

The Hermetic Tradition

Writings attributed to Hermes Trismegistus embrace an enormous range of teaching, and have led to many different schools. The quotations which follow have been taken from *The Occult Way* and *Sayings of the Ancient One*[4] by P. G. Bowen, who followed A.E. (George Russell) as President of the Hermetic Society of Dublin. They possess an outstandingly precise, though cryptic quality.

About God

In the beginning, Earth was without form and void, and Darkness covered the Great Deep. Then from Darkness a Voice sounds, sending its echoes throughout non-being, and these are the words which it speaks:

'I am all that was. I am all that is. I am all that is to be.

'I am all forms; all forms live in me, but All-Form is not I, but only my fleeting shadows.

'I am all power; all power moves in me, but All-Power is not I, but only my changing aspects.

'I am all wisdom; all wisdom shines in me, but All-Wisdom is not I, but only my fitful gleams.

'All knowledge, all power, all substance live in Me, and I am in them and manifest through them, but I am also above them, and beyond them, eternally unmanifest.'

Hermetic Invocation

Fundamental Principles

As is the Inner so is the Outer; as is the Great so is the Small; as it is Above so it is Below: there is but one Life and Law. Nothing is Inner, nothing is Outer; nothing is Great, nothing is Small; nothing is High, nothing is Low, in the Divine Economy.

Hermetic Axiom

Nothing is false; nothing is true; all things that exist are but masks of Truth; accept no thing; reject no thing; learn from study of all; but above all learn from the Learner.

The Mother lives by eternally restoring a balance that her children eternally destroy.

21

The vices of men become steps in the ladder, one by one as they are surmounted. The virtues of men are steps . . . but though they create a fair atmosphere and a happy future they are useless if they stand alone.

Rest upon no step however high; if you do it will change and become a snare.

Light on the Path

For within you is the light of the world – the only light that can be shed upon the Path. If you cannot see it within you it is useless to look for it elsewhere. It is beyond you; because when you have reached it you have lost yourself. It is unattainable because it for ever recedes. You will enter the light but you will never touch the flame.

Light on the Path

There are three truths which are absolute, and which cannot be lost, but yet may remain silent for lack of speech.

The soul of man is immortal, and its future is the future of a thing whose growth and splendour has no limit.

The principle which gives life dwells in us and without us, is undying and eternally beneficent, is not heard or seen, or smelt, but is perceived by the man who desires perception.

Each man is his own absolute lawgiver, the dispenser of glory or gloom to himself; the decreer of his life, his reward, his punishment.

These truths, which are as great as is life itself, are as simple as the simplest mind of man. Feed the hungry with them.

Idyll of the White Lotus

Application

Labour always like one who seeks a Royal Reward for a task well done; but find your reward in work continued and never in work completed.

Rejoice if your lot is happy; but if it is miserable rejoice also: Joy and Sadness are your twin slaves joined from birth, and they must serve you together or serve you not at all.

Love Life, for he is the Great teacher; but love Death also, for he is the other Self of Life, who alone can teach you nothing.

Regard your five senses as tax-gatherers to a king, for they bring you toll of the wealth of your kingdom, but beware lest the spoils they collect deceive you and cause you to forget that they are but tithes.

He saw the lightning in the East, and longed for the East; had he seen it in the West he would have longed for the West; but I, seeking only the Lightning and its Glory, care nothing for the Quarters of the Earth.

An Allegory

If you voyage with the stream of true Waters you will reach six different ports, and these are their names: Light, Strength, Peace, Wealth, Self, Wisdom.

True Light lies hidden behind Giant Rocks, and its only approach is through the Caverns of Mind.

True Strength is encompassed by demons called Powers, and cannot be gained until they are slain.

True Peace is encircled by seething whirlpools, and can be entered only while Tempests rage.

True Wealth is enshrouded by Shadows called Possessions, and cannot be gained until they are scattered.

True Self is masked by countless reflections, and cannot be sighted until they are washed away.

True Wisdom has no shadows, and is found in Sunlit Waters when all other ports are passed.

Buddhism

In relation to Buddhism serious difficulties are presented by the extent of present texts and commentaries, and the time which elapsed between the death of the Buddha and the first *written* texts. Before these appeared, everything depended on oral tradition. It follows that selecting passages which record correctly what the Buddha actually said is extremely hazardous! At the same time much of the Buddha's teaching centres round certain major themes, so that his reported discourses which refer to these themes in a direct and simple manner are unlikely to differ significantly from what he actually said. The passages quoted have been chosen with this in mind. Unless stated otherwise, they have been taken from *Some Sayings of the Buddha, according to the Pali Canon*, by F. L. Woodward.[5]

Included as an Appendix are the *Twelve Principles of Buddhism*, a statement which was prepared shortly after the end of World War II and has the general agreement of many of today's Buddhist schools.[6]

Statements made by Gautama, the Buddha, about himself

I, brethren, when I so desire it, can call to mind my various states of birth . . . I lived there, was named thus, was of such a clan, of such a caste, was thus supported, had such and such pleasant and painful experiences, had such a length of days, disappeared thence and arose elsewhere: there too I lived, was named thus, was of such a clan, of such a caste – thus can I call to mind in all their specific details, in all their characteristics, in many various ways, my previous states of existence.

The Exalted One, taking up a handful of simsapa leaves, said to the brethren:
'Which are more, these few simsapa leaves that I hold in my hand, or those that are in the simsapa grove above?'
'Few in number, Lord, are those simsapa leaves that are in the hand of the Exalted One: far more in number are those in the simsapa grove above.'
'Just so, brethren, those things that I know by my super-knowledge, but have not revealed, are greater by far in number than those things that I have revealed. And why, brethren, have I not revealed them? Because, brethren, they do not conduce to profit, are not concerned with the holy life, they do not tend to repulsion, to cessation, to calm, to the super-knowledge, to the perfect wisdom, to Nirvana. That is why I have not revealed them.'

Fundamental Principles

All that we are is the result of what we have thought.

Dammapada 1

24

Now this, brethren, is the Ariyan Truth about Suffering:

Birth is Suffering, Decay is Suffering, Sickness is Suffering, Death is Suffering, likewise Sorrow and Grief, Woe, Lamentation and Despair. To be conjoined with things which we dislike, to be separated from things which we like – that also is Suffering. Not to get what one wants – that also is Suffering. In a word, this Body, this five-fold mass which is based on Grasping, that is Suffering. Now this, brethren, is the Ariyan Truth about *The Origin of Suffering*:

It is that *Craving* that leads downwards to birth, along with the Lure and the Lust that lingers longingly now here, now there: namely, the craving for Sensation, the Craving to be born again, the Craving to have done with rebirth. Such, brethren, is the Ariyan Truth about *The Origin of Suffering*.

And this, brethren, is the Ariyan Truth about *The Ceasing of Suffering*:

Verily it is the utter passionless cessation of, the giving up, the forsaking, the release from, the absence of longing for, this *Craving*.

Now this, brethren, is the Ariyan Truth about The Way leading to *The Ceasing of Suffering*. Verily it is this Ariyan Eightfold Path, that is:

RIGHT VIEW, RIGHT AIM, RIGHT SPEECH, RIGHT ACTION, RIGHT LIVING, RIGHT EFFORT, RIGHT MINDFULNESS, RIGHT CONTEMPLATION.

Brethren, of deeds done and accumulated with deliberate intent I declare there is no wiping out. That wiping out has to come to pass either in this very life or in some other life at its proper occasion. Without experiencing the results of deeds so done, I declare there is no making an end of ill.

Application

These two extremes, brethren, should not be followed by one who has gone forth as a wanderer:

Devotion to the pleasures of sense – a low and pagan practice, unworthy, unprofitable, the way of the world on the one hand, and on the other hand devotion to self-mortification, which is painful, unworthy, unprofitable.

By avoiding these two extremes He who hath won the Truth

has gained knowledge of that *Middle Path* which giveth Vision, which giveth Knowledge, which causeth Calm, Insight, Enlightenment, and Nirvana.

And what is that *Middle Path*?

Verily it is this Ariyan Eightfold Path, that is to say:

RIGHT VIEW, RIGHT AIM, RIGHT SPEECH, RIGHT
ACTION, RIGHT LIVING, RIGHT EFFORT, RIGHT
MINDFULNESS, RIGHT CONTEMPLATION.

Now what, brethren, is RIGHT VIEW?

The Knowledge about Ill, the Arising of Ill, the Ceasing of Ill, and the Way leading to the Ceasing of Ill, – that, brethren, is called Right View.

And what, brethren, is RIGHT AIM?

The being set on Renunciation, on Non-resentment, on Harmlessness, – that, brethren, is called Right Aim.

And what, brethren, is RIGHT SPEECH?

Abstinence from lying speech, from backbiting and abusive speech, and from idle babble, – that, brethren, is called Right Speech.

And what, brethren, is RIGHT ACTION?

Abstinence from taking life, from taking what is not given, from wrong-doing in sexual passions, – that, brethren, is called Right Action.

And what, brethren, is RIGHT LIVING?

Herein, brethren, the Ariyan disciple, by giving up wrong living, gets his livelihood by right living, – that, brethren, is called Right Living.

And what, brethren, is RIGHT EFFORT?

Herein, brethren, a brother generates the will to inhibit the arising of evil immoral conditions that have not yet arisen: he makes an effort, he sets energy afoot, he applies his mind and struggles. Likewise (he does the same) to reject evil immoral conditions that have already arisen. Likewise (he does the same) to cause the arising of good conditions that have not yet arisen. Likewise (he does the same) to establish, to prevent the corruption, to cause the increase, the practice, the fulfilment of good conditions that have already arisen. This, brethren, is called Right Effort.

And what, brethren, is RIGHT MINDFULNESS?

Herein, brethren, a brother dwells regarding body as a

compound, he dwells ardent, self possessed, recollected, by controlling the covetousness and dejection that are in the world. So also with regard to Feelings, with regard to Perception, with regard to the Activities, with regard to Thought. This, brethren, is called Right Mindfulness.

Abstention from all evil, doing of what is skilled, purification of one's thought – this is the doctrine of the Buddhas.

I taught you not to believe merely because you have heard, but when you believed of your consciousness, then to act accordingly and abundantly.

Work out your own salvation – with diligence.

A Parable

Once the Exalted One was staying near Savatthi. A number of sectarians, recluses, and brahmins who were wanderers, entered Savatthi to beg an alms: they were men of divers faith, of divers aims, and by divers opinions swayed to and fro. And each maintained that his own view was the truth, and that all else was delusion.

Then said the Exalted One:

'These sectarians, brethren, are blind and unseeing. They know not the real, they know not the unreal, know not the truth, know not the untruth: in such a state of ignorance do they dispute and quarrel.

'In former times, brethren, there was a rajah in this same Savatthi. Then, brethren, that rajah called to a certain man, saying: "Go and gather together all the blind men that are in Savatthi." That man, in obedience to the rajah gathered together all the blind men. "Your Majesty, all the blind men of Savatthi are now assembled." "Then, my good man, show these blind men an elephant."

'"Very good, your majesty," said the man, and did as he was told, saying, "Oh ye blind, such as this is an elephent."

'And to one man he presented the head of the elephant, to another the ear, to another a tusk, the trunk, the foot, back, tail, and tuft of the tail, saying to each one that that was the elephant.

'Thereupon, brethren, that rajah went up to the blind men

27

and said to each, "Have you studied the elephant?" "Yes, your majesty." "Then tell me your conclusions about him."

'Thereupon those who had been presented with the head answered, "Your majesty, an elephant is just like a pot." And those who had only observed the ear replied, "An elephant is just like a winnowing-basket." Those who had been presented with the tusk said it was a ploughshare. Those who knew only the trunk said it was a plough. "The body," said they, "is a granary: the foot, a pillar: the back, a mortar: its tail, a pestle: the tuft of the tail, just a besom." Then they began to quarrel, shouting, "Yes, it is. No, it isn't." And so on, till they came to fisticuffs.

'Just so are these sectarians, blind, unseeing, knowing not the truth, but each maintaining it is thus and thus.'

Twelve Principles of Buddhism

1. Self-salvation is for any man the immediate task. If a man lay wounded by a poisoned arrow he would not delay extraction by demanding details of the man who shot it, or the length and make of the arrow. There will be time for ever-increasing understanding of the Teaching during the treading of the Way. Meanwhile, begin now by facing life as it is, learning always by direct and personal experience.

2. The first fact of existence is the law of change or impermanence. All that exists, from a mole to a mountain, from a thought to an empire, passes through the same cycle of existence – i.e. birth, growth, decay and death. Life alone is continuous, ever seeking self-expression in new forms. 'Life is a bridge; therefore build no house on it.' Life is a process of flow, and he who clings to any form, however splendid, will suffer by resisting the flow.

3. The law of change applies equally to the 'soul'. There is no principle in an individual which is immortal and unchanging. Only the 'namelessness', the ultimate Reality, is beyond change, and all forms of life,

28

including man, are manifestations of this Reality. No one owns the life which flows in him any more than the electric light bulb owns the current which gives it light.

4. The universe is the expression of law. All effects have causes, and man's soul or character is the sum total of his previous thoughts and acts. Karma, meaning action-reaction, governs all existence, and man is the sole creator of his circumstances and his reaction to them, his future condition and his final destiny. By right thought and action he can gradually purify his inner nature, and so by self-realisation attain in time liberation from rebirth. The process covers great periods of time, involving life after life on earth, but ultimately every form of life will reach Enlightenment.

5. Life is one indivisible, though its ever-changing forms are innumerable and perishable. There is, in truth, no death, though every form must die. From an understanding of life's unity arises compassion, a sense of identity with the life in other forms. Compassion is described as 'the Law of laws – eternal harmony', and he who breaks this harmony of life will suffer accordingly and delay his own Enlightenment.

6. Life being One, the interests of the part should be those of the whole. In his ignorance man thinks he can successfully strive for his own interests, and this wrongly-directed energy of selfishness produces suffering. He learns from his suffering to reduce and finally eliminate its cause. The Buddha taught four Noble Truths: (a) The omnipresence of suffering; (b) its cause, wrongly directed desire; (c) its cure, the removal of the cause; and (d) the Noble Eightfold Path of self-development which leads to the end of suffering.

7. The Eightfold Path consists in Right (or perfect) Views or preliminary understanding, Right Aims or Motive, Right Speech, Right Acts, Right Livelihood, Right Effort, Right Concentration or mind-development,

and, finally, Right Samadhi, leading to full Enlightenment. As Buddhism is a way of living, not merely a theory of life, the treading of this Path is essential to self-deliverance. 'Cease to do evil, learn to do good, cleanse your own heart: this is the Teaching of the Buddhas.'

8. Reality is indescribable, and a God with attributes is not the final Reality. But the Buddha, a human being, became the All-Enlightened One, and the purpose of life is the attainment of Enlightenment. This state of Consciousness, Nirvana, the extinction of the limitations of selfhood, is attainable on earth. All men and all other forms of life contain the potentiality of Enlightenment, and the process therefore consists in becoming what you are, 'Look within: thou art Buddha.'

9. From potential to actual Enlightenment there lies the Middle Way, the Eightfold Path 'from desire to peace', a process of self-development between the 'opposites', avoiding all extremes. The Buddha trod this Way to the end, and the only faith required in Buddhism is the reasonable belief that where a Guide has trodden it is worth our while to tread. The Way must be trodden by the whole man, not merely the best of him, and heart and mind must be developed equally. The Buddha was the All-Compassionate as well as the All-Enlightened One.

10. Buddhism lays great stress on the need of inward concentration and meditation, which leads in time to the development of the inner spiritual faculties. The subjective life is as important as the daily round, and periods of quietude for inner activity are essential for a balanced life. The Buddhist should at all times be 'mindful and self-possessed', refraining from mental and emotional attachment to 'the passing show'. This increasingly watchful attitude to circumstances, which he knows to be his own creation, helps him to keep his reaction to it always under control.

11. The Buddha said: 'Work out your own salvation with diligence.' Buddhism knows no authority for truth save the intuition of the individual, and that is authority for himself alone. Each man suffers the consequences of his own acts, and learns thereby, while helping his fellow men to the same deliverance; nor will prayer to the Buddha or to any God prevent an effect from following its cause. Buddhist monks are teachers and exemplars, and in no sense intermediates between Reality and the individual. The utmost tolerance is practised towards all other religions and philosophies, for no man has the right to interfere in his neighbour's journey to the Goal.

12. Buddhism is neither pessimistic nor 'escapist', nor does it deny the existence of God or soul, though it places its own meaning on these terms. It is, on the contrary, a system of thought, a religion, a spiritual science and a way of life, which is reasonable, practical and all-embracing. For over two thousand years it has satisfied the spiritual needs of nearly one-third of mankind. It appeals to the West because it has no dogmas, satisfies the reason and the heart alike, insists on self-reliance coupled with tolerance for other points of view, embraces science, religion, philosophy, psychology, ethics and art, and points to man alone as the creator of his present life and sole designer of his destiny.

Christianity

Here, the same difficulty exists as in the case of Buddhism, though not in such an acute form. According to the experts, the appearance of the first Gospel, that of Mark, was probably not until thirty or forty years after the death and resurrection of Jesus. Though this is not a long period compared with the two thousand years of the Christian era, much can get distorted or be forgotten in a period of thirty or forty years, and care must therefore be exercised regarding the weight placed on a particular saying. The choice of the passages quoted must inevitably be open to criticism, but it is hoped that they embody the heart of what Jesus actually said and taught. It is, of course, realised that very little is said about the crucifixion, death and resurrection – what many Christians regard as the essence of Christianity – because the quoted passages have been selected from what Jesus is recorded as having said, not from the descriptive accounts of others. A particular problem is posed by the meditations of Jesus recorded in John. It is inconceivable that what Jesus is reported to have said (if, indeed, he actually *said* anything) would have been in the presence of, let alone audible to, a bystander. (cf. Matthew 6:6) But what is recorded in the Gospel has an underlying authority which is unmistakable.

In what follows, unless indicated by the letters A.V. (Authorised Version), the Biblical quotations are all taken from the Revised Version.

About God

No man hath seen God at any time.

John 1:18

God is Spirit: and they that worship him must worship in spirit and truth.

John 4:24

Why callest thou me good? None is good save one, even God.

Mark 10:18

Statements made by Jesus about his relationship with God

For God so loved the world, that he gave his only begotten Son, that whosoever believeth in him should not perish, but have eternal life.

John 3:16

For I am come down from heaven, not to do mine own will, but the will of him that sent me.

John 4:38

32

EVIDENCE FROM THE SCRIPTURES

Before Abraham was, I am.

John 8:58

I and the Father are one.

John 10:30

The Father is in me, and I in the Father.

John 10:38

I am the way, and the truth, and the life: no one cometh unto the Father, but by me.

John 14:6

If ye loved me, ye would have rejoiced, because I go unto the Father: for the Father is greater than I.

John 14:28

To this end was I born, and for this cause came I into the world, that I should bear witness unto the truth.

John 18:37 (A.V.)

Father, if thou be willing, remove this cup from me: nevertheless not my will, but thine, be done.

Luke 22:42

Father, forgive them; for they know not what they do.

Luke 23:34

My God, my God, why hast thou forsaken me?

Matthew 27:46

Fundamental Principles

I am the light of the world: he that followeth me shall not walk in the darkness, but shall have the light of life.

John 8:12

He that believeth on me, the works that I do shall he do also, and greater works than these shall he do.

John 14:12

My Kingdom is not of this world.

John 18:36

Ask, and it shall be given you; seek, and ye shall find; knock, and it shall be opened unto you: for everyone that asketh

33

receiveth; and he that seeketh findeth; and to him that knocketh it shall be opened.

Matthew 7:7, 8

He that findeth his life shall lose it; and he that loseth his life for my sake shall find it.

Matthew 10:39

Whereunto shall I liken the kingdom of God? It is like unto leaven, which a woman took and hid in three measures of meal, till it was all leavened.

Luke 13:20, 21

The kingdom of God cometh not with observation: neither shall they say, Lo, here! or, There! for lo, the kingdom of God is within you.

Luke 17:21

The first is; the Lord our God, the Lord is one: and thou shalt love the Lord thy God with all thy heart, and with all thy soul, and with all thy mind, and with all thy strength. The second is this, Thou shalt love thy neighbour as thyself. There is none other commandment greater than these.

Mark 12:29–31

For with what measure ye mete it shall be measured to you again.

Luke 6:38; cf. Matthew 7:2; cf. Mark 4:24

Ye therefore shall be perfect, as your heavenly Father is perfect.

Matthew 5:48

Verily, verily I say unto thee, Except a man be born anew, he cannot see the Kingdom of God. Nicodemus saith unto him, How can a man be born when he is old? can he enter a second time into his mother's womb, and be born? Jesus answered, Verily, verily, I say unto thee, Except a man be born of water and the Spirit, he cannot enter into the kingdom of God. That which is born of the flesh is flesh; and that which is born of the Spirit is spirit.

John 3:3–6

34

In my Father's house are many mansions; if it were not so, I would have told you.

John 14:2

I have yet many things to say unto you, but ye cannot bear them now.

John 16:12

Application

Blessed are the poor in spirit: for theirs is the kingdom of heaven.
Blessed are they that mourn: for they shall be comforted.
Blessed are the meek: for they shall inherit the earth.
Blessed are they which do hunger and thirst after righteousness: for they shall be filled.
Blessed are the merciful: for they shall obtain mercy.
Blessed are the pure in heart: for they shall see God.
Blessed are the peacemakers: for they shall be called the children of God.
Blessed are they which are persecuted for righteousness' sake: for theirs is the kingdom of heaven.
Blessed are ye, when men shall revile you, and persecute you, and shall say all manner of evil against you falsely, for my sake. Rejoice, and be exceeding glad: for great is your reward in heaven: for so persecuted they the prophets which were before you.

Matthew 5:3–12 (AV)

Ye have heard that it hath been said, Thou shalt love thy neighbour, and hate thine enemy. But I say unto you, Love your enemies, bless them that curse you, do good to them that hate you, and pray for them which despitefully use you, and persecute you; that ye may be the children of your Father which is in heaven.

Matthew 5:43–45

But thou, when thou prayest, enter into thy closet, and when thou has shut thy door, pray to thy Father which is in secret; and thy Father which seeth in secret shall reward thee openly. But when ye pray, use not vain repetitions, as the heathen do: for they think that they shall be heard for their much speaking.

Be not ye therefore like unto them: for your Father knoweth what things ye have need of, before ye ask him. After this manner therefore pray ye:

Our Father which art in heaven, Hallowed be thy name. Thy Kingdom come. Thy will be done in earth, as it is in heaven. Give us this day our daily bread. And forgive us our debts, as we forgive our debtors. And lead us not into temptation, but deliver us from evil: For thine is the kingdom, and the power and the glory, for ever. Amen.

Matthew 6:6–15 (A.V.)

No man can serve two masters: for either he will hate the one, and love the other; or else he will hold to the one and despise the other. Ye cannot serve God and mammon. Therefore I say unto you, Be not anxious for your life, what ye shall eat, or what ye shall drink; nor yet for your body, what ye shall put on. Is not the life more than the food, and the body than the raiment? . . . Consider the lilies of the field, how they grow; they toil not, neither do they spin: yet I say unto you, that even Solomon in all is glory was not arrayed like one of these. But if God doth so clothe the grass of the field, which today is, and tomorrow is cast into the oven, shall he not much more clothe you, O ye of little faith?

Matthew 6:24, 25, 28, 30

Therefore whosoever heareth these sayings of mine, and doeth them, I will liken him unto a wise man, which built his house upon a rock: and the rain descended, and the floods came, and the winds blew, and beat upon that house; and it fell not: for it was founded upon a rock. And every one that heareth these sayings of mine, and doeth them not, shall be likened unto a foolish man, which built his house upon the sand: and the rain descended, and the floods came, and the winds blew, and beat upon that house; and it fell: and great was the fall of it.

Matthew 7:24–27 (A.V.)

A Parable

A certain man had two sons: and the younger of them said to his father, Father, give me the portion of thy substance that falleth to me. And he divided unto them his living. And not many days after the younger son gathered all together, and took his journey into a far country; and there he wasted his substance with riotous living. And when he had spent all, there arose a mighty famine in that country; and he began to be in want. And he went and joined himself to one of the citizens of that country; and he sent him into his fields to feed swine. And he would fain have been filled with the husks that the swine did eat: and no man gave unto him. But when he came to himself he said, How many hired servants of my father's have bread enough and to spare, and I perish here with hunger! I will arise and go to my father, and will say unto him, Father, I have sinned against heaven, and in thy sight: I am no more worthy to be called thy son: make me as one of thy hired servants. And he arose, and came to his father. But while he was yet afar off, his father saw him, and was moved with compassion, and ran, and fell on his neck, and kissed him. And the son said unto him, Father, I have sinned against heaven, and in thy sight: I am no more worthy to be called thy son. But the father said to his servants, Bring forth quickly the best robe, and put it on him; and put a ring on his hand, and shoes on his feet: and bring the fatted calf, and kill it, and let us eat, and make merry: for this my son was dead, and is alive again; he was lost, and is found. And they began to be merry. Now his elder son was in the field: and as he came and drew nigh to the house, he heard music and dancing. And he called to him one of the servants, and inquired what these things might be. And he said unto him, Thy brother is come; and thy father hath killed the fatted calf, because he hath received him safe and sound. But he was angry, and would not go in: and his father came out, and entreated him. But he answered and said to his father, Lo, these many years do I serve thee, and I never transgressed a commandment of thine: and yet thou never gavest me a kid, that I might make merry with my friends: but when this thy son came, which hath devoured thy living with harlots, thou killedst for him the fatted calf. And he said unto him, Son, thou art ever with me, and all that is mine is thine. But it was meet to make merry and be glad: for this thy brother was dead, and is alive again; and was lost, and is found.

Luke 15:11–32

References

1. *Bhagavad Gita*, translated with an introduction and commentary by Charles Johnston, (John M. Watkins, 1965)
2. *The Yoga Sutras of Patanjali*, an interpretation by Charles Johnston, (J. M. Watkins, 1949)
3. *The Light of the Soul – the Yoga Sutras of Patanjali*, by Alice Bailey, (Lucis Publishing Co., 1927)
4. (a) *The Occult Way*, by P. G. Bowen, (The Occult Book Society, 1938, republished by the Theosophical Publishing House)
   (b) *The Sayings of the Ancient One*, by P. G. Bowen, (Rider & Co., 1935, republished by the Theosophical Publishing House)
5. *Some Sayings of the Buddha, according to the Pali Canon*, translated by F. L. Woodward, (O.U.P., 1939)
6. *Buddhism*, by Christmas Humphreys, (Pelican, 1951), p. 74

4: Framing a Hypothesis

The first impression given by the quotations in the previous chapter is the difference in style and content. The second is the extent to which they are complementary, and not conflicting. Something that certainly cannot be said of today's formulated systems of belief.

The three questions posed in Chapter 2 were: Who or what is God? Who or what is man? What is the purpose of human life? We will start by seeing what light is shed on these questions by the quotations in Chapter 3.

In relation to the first question 'Who or what is God?', there emerge three distinct concepts. First, the Godhead, THAT from which all that is proceeds. This is described – in so far as description is possible – in the magnificent Hermetic Invocation (p. 21) (cf. the first five verses of St. John's Gospel which may well come from a comparable source), the famous passage from Book 8 of the Gita (p. 16), and perhaps – perhaps because the precise meaning is uncertain – some of Jesus' sayings recorded in St John's Gospel. Second, God as a Being – within the purely human context, a Supreme Being. Such is referred to as Krishna in the Gita, and on many occasions when Jesus referred to God as Father. Third, God immanent, God as the divine spark within every man. This is a fundamental tenet of Hinduism, and is suggested by some of the sayings of Jesus; St Paul stated it explicitly.[1] Though certain traditions may be silent, notably Buddhism, there is no obvious conflict.

The next question is 'Who or what is man?' About this all four traditions are unanimous in proclaiming in their own distinctive way that man is a self-conscious centre of life with

39

a potentially great future. The Hermetic Tradition asserts that the soul of man is immortal, and that its future is the future of a thing whose growth and splendour has no limit. (Soul here denotes the spiritual part of man; not to be confused with the more restrictive definition on p. 46.) In the Hindu and Buddhist traditions human destiny is *realisation* – attaining Nirvana (which is *not* annihilation, but a state of consciousness, bliss, which transcends physical sensing, emotional feeling, and discursive thinking, and is so remote from ordinary consciousness as to be virtually indescribable). In the Christian tradition, the son, the prodigal, returns to his Father's House. There is also the injunction 'Ye therefore shall be perfect as your heavenly Father is perfect'.

Though the preceding paragraph is relevant to the question, 'Who or what is man?', it does not answer it. And this, to the best of our ability, we must now try to do. Is man his physical body, and just that, or is he something more? And where does the 'I' – the sense of I-ness – stand in relation to feeling and thinking? Are feelings and thoughts part of the 'I', or not? By way of answer a clear lead is given by the *Aphorisms of Patanjali*, especially the one which states: 'The transfer of the consciousness from a lower vehicle into a higher is part of the great creative and evolutionary process.' This implies that to begin with man identifies himself with his physical body which thus appears to be himself. As man begins to appreciate that he is not his physical body – that his physical body is an instrument to be trained and used, an instrument, moreover, which has a life of its own, as shown by the presence of the physical appetites – it becomes objective and part of the not-self. According to Patanjali similar reasoning applies to man's emotional body (the name given to the emotional 'matter' that renders feeling possible) and man's mental body (the name given to the mental 'matter', chitta or mindstuff, that makes discursive thinking possible). As in the case of man's physical body, his emotional and mental bodies have a life of their own. The life of the former is demonstrated by the use of such phrases as 'I lost my temper', 'I was overwhelmed by jealousy', 'I was overcome by fear'. The life of the latter by the extreme difficulty which everyone has in keeping their mind fixed, without wavering, on something which is devoid of intrinsic interest. And the quality of these bodies – whether coarse or refined – will largely determine the quality of the feelings and thoughts – whether coarse or refined – which can manifest by means of them. Hence the wisdom of St Paul's famous passage:

> Whatsoever things are true, whatsoever things are honourable, whatsoever things are just, whatsoever things are lovely, whatsoever things are of good report, if there be any virtue and if there be any praise, think on these things.[2]

Modern physics has shown that matter and energy are interconnected, so that when we talk about the physical body, we are talking about an intensely complex energy pattern within a certain range of energies. And the same is true for the emotional and mental bodies, albeit the range of energies is different. In time, Patanjali asserts, man will come to regard his emotional and mental bodies as objective and part of the not-self, in the same way that he is now coming to regard his physical body. They are instruments, for him to train and use. The shift in consciousness which this involves eventually leads to a realisation of the Self, the centre which transcends physical sensing, emotional feeling and discursive thinking.

This approach receives considerable confirmation, albeit in a totally different idiom, from the teaching of Jesus about the Kingdom of Heaven. Jesus' statement that 'The Kingdom of Heaven is within you' implies that the Kingdom is a state of consciousness, an interpretation which is confirmed by the parable of the leaven which 'a woman took and hid in three measures of meal, till it was all leavened', i.e. until the physical, emotional, and mental natures were all permeated by the spirit. About how this shift in consciousness is to be brought about, all four traditions have much to say, and little, if any, conflicts. Indeed, the existence of this heightened awareness – Nirvana in the Hindu and Buddhist traditions, the Kingdom of Heaven in the Christian – and how to attain it, constitutes the very heart of the religious message in all four traditions. The personal ego – the 'I' in 'I wish or I want, or I don't wish or I don't want, for myself' – has to be deposed, and subsumed in something greater than itself.

The Buddha's approach to the problem is by analysing the cause of suffering. He points out that personal desire, either for what one wants but has not got or for what one has got but does not want, causes suffering, and that the only way to avoid it is by giving up wanting, 'the utter passionless cessation of, the giving up, the forsaking, the release from, the absence of longing for this craving'. And to achieve this the Buddha unfolds the eightfold path – right view, right aim, right speech, right action, right living, right effort, right mindfulness, right contemplation. The first six steps are concerned with refining the personality, the last two with transcending it.

In the Gita reference is made to a number of paths, three in particular. But all involve the transformation of personal desire, and its replacement by what is referred to as soul-vision and non-attachment. The abstract path for 'those who worship the Eternal, undefined, unmanifest, omnipresent', the foundation of all that is, is 'hard for mortals to attain'. Of the other two paths, one is characterised by love of Ishvara (God as a personal Being); the other by works, when these are performed in a spirit of total detachment: 'Thy right is to the work, but never to its fruits; let not the fruit of thy work be thy motive'. These three paths are described in detail in works on Jnana Yoga (the path of knowledge, wisdom), Bhakti Yoga (the path of devotion), and Karma Yoga (the Yoga of action). But all three paths lead to the same goal, the transcendence of the personal consciousness and the attainment of Nirvana.

42

The *Aphorisms of Patanjali* refer to a fourth path, Raja Yoga, in which the will is the vital factor, and the dominant characteristic is control: first of the physical body, then of the emotions, and finally of the mind. This, too, leads to Nirvana.

In its allegorical and cryptic way, the Hermetic Tradition proclaims the same message. The injunction 'Labour always like one who seeks a Royal Reward for a task well done; but find your reward in work continued and never in work completed' is remarkably similar to the Gita 'Thy right is to the work, but never to its fruits'. And the allegory about 'The Stream of True Waters' has its parallel in the obstacles to be overcome as described in Patanjali's Aphorisms. About the transformation of personal desire and the spiritual consciousness to which this leads, P. G. Bowen, who was deeply versed in the Hermetic Philosophy, writes as follows:

> The great, ever-present problem confronting all who set themselves to travel this path is the conquest of desire. The more it is considered, the more difficult does it appear to one who thinks, but still lacks clear understanding. Desire, he perceives, is the great motive power of life, and if it be destroyed what can take its place? Without desire he thinks, and thinks rightly, there would be apathy and stagnation, but he fails to understand that DESIRE as a principle in universal nature is utterly different from human desires. The Desire Principle can no more be eliminated than can the universe, but human desires are simply the self-isolated consciousness functioning within this principle.
>
> At this point it should be clearly understood that the spiritual, or universal consciousness which disciples, initiates, and Masters exercise in one degree or another is not merely an extension of the personal human variety, but is of a different, and higher nature altogether. Cultivation of personal powers and faculties, no matter how intense, will never transform personal man into the disciple. It may, and usually does, check his progress towards the spiritual life, just as over-development of the animal nature inhibits evolution of higher human

43

qualities in the child. This does not mean that human faculties, among which intellect is predominant, should be neglected. They are all instruments of experience, and only through experience is wisdom gained. . . .

But just as no man can describe to another who has not seen it the miracle of the dawn of an earthly day, so can no words convey to the personal mind what waking to spiritual consciousness means. To be known it must be experienced. Nothing more can be said.[3]

Coming now to the teaching of Jesus recorded in the Gospels, three themes stand out regarding the question 'Who or what is man?' First the necessity for repentance, metanoia, a change in attitude of mind. Second, the need summarised by the injunction – 'Seek ye first his Kingdom (a state of heightened awareness) and his righteousness; and all these things shall be added unto you.' Third, the method by which this heightened awareness is to be attained – 'By loving God, and thy neighbour as thyself.' In this context God is referred to as a loving Father; and to the question 'Who is my neighbour?', Jesus replied with the Parable of the Good Samaritan, i.e. everyman.

This brings us to the remaining question 'What is the purpose of human life?' The answer has already been largely provided when considering the nature of man: by the realisation that man has a spiritual nature, and that his destiny is to reveal this nature. In practice, this means that he should be able to fill whatever role he is called upon to play in ordinary life with grace, skill, and selfless dedication. But this raises a problem. For attaining Nirvana (Hinduism and Buddhism), or entering the Kingdom of Heaven (Christianity), and so becoming a Master of the Art and Science of Living, cf. Gautama or Jesus, is not to be accomplished overnight. As a matter of experience the progress that can be made in a single lifetime, even by the most determined and dedicated, is severely limited. How then is the goal to be achieved?

Consideration of this question leads to a parting of the

ways, with Hinduism and Buddhism indicating one way, and Christianity another. According to the former, progress is spread over many lives; in Christian teaching it is confined to one only. What are we to make of this?

In Hinduism and Buddhism references to a series of lives, to reincarnation, is quite explicit. In Christianity belief in the concept was formally anathematised by the Roman Emperor Justinian in 553. And the ban has remained. Reverting to the Gospels and the teaching of Jesus, there is virtually nothing, either in favour or against the concept. The most significant relevant saying is 'In whatsoever measure ye mete it shall be measured to you again,' a saying which is recorded in almost identical words in each of the first three Gospels. It is, in fact, very similar to the Hermetic statement: 'Each man is his own absolute lawgiver, the dispenser of glory or gloom to himself; the decreer of his life, his reward, his punishment.' As the concept of reincarnation was not unfamiliar at the time of Jesus, it is surprising that the Gospels contain no comment about the validity or otherwise of the idea. Such complete silence, coupled with the implication of the saying of Jesus just quoted, makes one wonder whether Jesus did, in fact, say *something*; but that on account of its unacceptability in certain quarters, what he said has been omitted, or perhaps deleted, from such written records as have come down to us. We simply do not know.

In Buddhism and Hinduism reincarnation is usually thought of in conjunction with karma, the law of ethical causation. In fact, reincarnation is regarded as a consequence of karma. Causes which originate in the three dimensional space-time world of the five physical senses must have their effects in that self same world. Put a little differently, what is sown in one field must be harvested from the *same* field. All *personal* desire 'binds', i.e. produces effects which must be experienced in our three dimensional space-time world. But as desire is transformed and the personal element fades, so too do the fetters which chain man to the material world of the five physical senses.

45

The saying of Jesus already quoted, 'In whatsoever measure ye mete it shall be measured to you again,' can be regarded as a very succinct statement of the law of karma, and raises the question of where and how reaping is to take place if not of the field in which the seed was sown? In what seems to be conventional Christian thinking the answer usually given is 'the next world', coupled with the thought that if the person concerned is sincerely repentant (about some sin or sins), he will be 'forgiven', and the consequences of what he did or thought will be annulled. Though proof (either way) is hard to come by, such a view does seem extraordinarily unsatisfactory. As an analogy consider a boy at school. Suppose that during one particular term he performs very badly and that his terminal report reflects this fact. The subsequent holidays will be affected, and may involve some remedial, and probably unwelcome, measures. But the term's failings can be made good, and can only be made good, by a subsequent term (or terms) in which the earlier shortcomings are *demonstrably* overcome.

In the Hermetic tradition karma has its counterpart in what is referred to as the 'Law of the Inevitable Consequence'. And the cosmic significance of balance, of which karma can be regarded as an aspect, is shown by the cryptic statement: 'The Mother lives by eternally restoring a balance that her children eternally destroy.'

If reincarnation is adopted as a working hypothesis, it becomes necessary to introduce a name for that which 'bridges' the divine spark, the atman, and the transient personality. No name is entirely satisfactory, but 'soul' seems to be the best available. It contains the distillate of all that has been learnt from previous forays into incarnation and exists on a level of consciousness which transcends physical sensing, emotional feeling, and discursive thinking.

We must now consider the quotations listed on pp. 32 *et seq.* – 'Statements made by Jesus about his relationship with God.' These sayings have no parallel in the other traditions and are clearly very important. As the problem posed by the question 'Who was Jesus; Who was Christ?' was considered in some detail in *The Sacred Quest*, what follows will be restricted to a summary of the thesis developed there.

The *indisputable* facts about the central figure in the Christian Gospel include –

> An outstanding religious teacher was born, and died, in Palestine about two thousand years ago.

> Knowledge about the first thirty years of his life is minimal.

> Much more is known – although uncertainty regarding details continues – about the period of his ministry, which culminated with his crucifixion at Jerusalem.

> Following his resurrection, he appeared in physical form to his disciples and others on a number of different occasions.

The above facts, together with the Gospel Story, prompt the following observations –

> During Jesus' childhood there is no hint that he was regarded as other than a normal boy, albeit exceptionally perceptive and intelligent.

> The nature of Jesus' ministry makes it inconceivable that he remained in the carpenter's shop at Nazareth until the time of his baptism by John.

> Jesus' ministry – what he taught and *the way he lived and died* – had such a consistently sublime quality that it is difficult to believe that he was purely human, using the word human in its normally accepted sense.

Bearing in mind the possibility of 'overshadowing',[4] it is *suggested* that Jesus was a high initiate who was overshadowed by, and on occasion lent his body to, the Christ – the Supreme Master who may, in turn and on occasion, have been overshadowed by the Cosmic Christ, the second aspect of the Lord of the World, the God of this planet. However strange this may seem to the reader meeting this idea for the first time, it does go some way to explain some singularly difficult features of the Gospel Story, to wit –

47

The human quality of Jesus' early years.

The sublime quality of Jesus' ministry.

The words spoken from the cross: 'My God, my God, why hast thou forsaken me?' These words would come, not from the Christ, but from Jesus, who was then undergoing the fourth initiation, usually referred to as the Crucifixion or Great Renunciation Initiation. According to at least one esoteric tradition Christ was undergoing a quite different but much higher initiation at the same time.[5]

Having reviewed the evidence arising from the foundations of the four religious traditions that we have been considering, it is now time to see whether we can formulate a working hypothesis which will coordinate and synthesise the data provided by these traditions. Since it is not possible to explain the higher in terms of the lower, (e.g. feeling in terms of sensing, or thinking in terms of feeling), use will be made of a number of allegories. No claim is made for their originality. Several of them are prompted by, or adapted from, ancient writings. If justification is looked for, a little is provided by the Hermetic Axiom (p. 21), and by the following statement in *The Secret Doctrine* by H. P. Blavatsky:

Analogy is the guiding law in Nature, the only true Ariadne's thread that can lead us, through the inexplicable paths of her domain, toward her primal and final mysteries.[6]

The working hypothesis proceeds from a reference to alpha, *the Godhead*, to a consideration of omega, *the End to which all life moves*, and comprises an invocation and four allegories. These are first stated and then enlarged upon.

A   *A (alpha), the Godhead. THAT from which all that is proceeds – The Hermetic Invocation.*

B   *Who or what is God? The relationship of God to man can be likened to that of a human being to the cells in his (or her) body.*

C   *Who or what is man? The constitution of man can be likened to that of a charioteer and the chariot which he (or she) is driving.*

D   *What is the purpose of human life? Human life can be likened to life at school – the learning of lessons in a school of spiritual development.*

E   *Ω (omega), the End to which all life moves. The End is an ever expanding and ever deepening consciousness – the Kingdom of Heaven, Nirvana.*

* * *

A   *A (alpha), the Godhead, THAT from which all that is proceeds – The Hermetic Invocation. (p.21)*

About the manifestation of THAT, P. G. Bowen has this to say.

> BEING (or any Being) in ultimate metaphysical analysis is a compound of three elements, CONSCIOUSNESS, ENERGY, and SUBSTANCE, no one of which has any independent manifestation, or is knowable, otherwise than in interaction with the other two. All three exist in everything – in every aspect of LIFE, whether that aspect is perceived objectively through the senses or subjectively as an image in Consciousness.
>
> Is THAT a Self-conscious Being? It cannot be, for THAT is infinite, and Being implies limitation. THAT is the ONE, the only true, SELF. In THAT, all Beings have their Noumenon.[7]

B   *Who or what is God? The relationship of God to man can be likened to that of a human being to the cells in his (or her) body.*

The human body consists of millions upon millions of cells. They are of many different kinds and have many different functions. But all are conscious, i.e. have the capacity to be aware and to respond, though they are not, of course, self-conscious. In some strange way there is within the human body a hierarchy of beings. Few cells function independently, nearly all function as one of a small (relative to the totality of cells) group, e.g. to form a muscle. Nor are most small groups independent. In conjunction with other small groups they function as part of a larger group, e.g. the heart. Proceeding in this way we eventually arrive at the (human and self-conscious) being whose consciousness informs the entire body. In this picture there are several points of interest.

Until we arrive at the (human and self-conscious) being whose consciousness informs the whole body, all lesser beings are part of something greater than themselves. Harmony prevails, i.e. the body functions as it is intended to function, if every being in the body, whether humble like the cell or exalted like the heart, fulfils its responsibilities, i.e. performs efficiently its rightful function, and is afforded its rights, i.e. the conditions under which it can perform efficiently its rightful function. Disharmony occurs when some being in the body no longer fulfils its responsibilities, with the result that the body no longer functions as it should. An obvious example is cancer. In colloquial terms the cancer cells kick over the traces and embark on a policy of ruthless self-aggrandisement. In due course this leads to either the destruction of the cells concerned, together probably with a host of 'innocent' cells as well, or to a condition in which the body can no longer function and there is death.

The most significant feature of this allegory is the manner and extent to which the hierarchy of beings is *interdependent*. No being exists for itself and itself alone; each influences directly what is 'below', and limits the manifestation of what is 'above'. Moreover, the picture provided by this allegory indicates the existence of *many levels* of awareness, and so suggests the possibility for many of *many* levels of consciousness. Could it be that in this allegory the Christ corresponds to the heart?

C *Who or what is man? The constitution of man can be likened to that of a charioteer and the chariot which he (or she) is driving.*

Observing a chariot, ready for action, we notice the following. First, the ground over which the chariot is to be driven and which looks in places fairly rough. Second, the actual chariot. Third, the horses – two of them and full of life. Fourth, the reins – two pairs, one for each horse. Fifth,

50

the charioteer. Sixth, standing in the chariot behind the charioteer, the captain. Seventh, the commander. Eighth, but in the background, the ruler.

In this allegory, the route to be taken by the chariot is life's journey, on which the going is sometimes easy and sometimes hard. The chariot is the physical body which it is essential to keep in good repair. For when the going is rough, the bolts, bearings, and material of which the chariot is made will all be subject to severe testing. The horses are the emotions, the driving force without which we get nowhere. The reins correspond to the discursive intellect, almost the only way by which we control our emotions. The right hand horse and the reins by which it is controlled symbolise that subtle combination of feeling and thinking which constitutes 'desire for' something or someone. The left hand horse and the reins by which it is controlled symbolise that equally subtle combination of feeling and thinking which constitutes 'aversion from' someone or something. The charioteer is the 'I'; the captain represents the soul. The commander is in charge of a fleet of chariots of which the chariot we are looking at is one. The ruler is the one for whom the fleet of chariots exists.

In this picture there are several features which merit attention. The importance of ensuring that the actual chariot (the physical body) is in good condition is obvious. But equally, if not more, important is the condition of the horses (the emotional nature). The key word here is control, not to be confused with stifle. If the charioteer is to perform his task successfully, his horses must be strong, active, and responsive. This means that they must be well fed, trained and exercised. If the horses are inadequately fed, they will not be up to the work to be done. If they are fed but not exercised, they are likely to become unmanageable. To achieve the desired control, skilled manipulation of the reins is fundamental. Lack of the required skill leads to the horses taking the chariot whither it should not go. (cf. St Paul's heartfelt observation, 'For the good which I would I do not:

51

but the evil which I would not, that I practise.')[8] Great skill is also required in getting the two horses with their very different temperaments to pull together. (cf. The Buddhist middle path between 'desire for', and 'aversion from', someone or something.)

For most of us, learning to drive a chariot is so all-absorbing – the reins become tangled and the horses get out of control – that for much of the time we are oblivious of the captain and quite unable to follow his directions. But after many failures and much hard work and practice, a certain mastery is achieved, and the charioteer is able to listen to and follow, at least in some measure, his captain's directions. A more advanced stage of instruction then becomes possible. Realisation dawns of the existence of the commander and the fleet of chariots under his command, and the rapport between charioteer and captain becomes increasingly close. Between periods of practice the captain will discuss with the charioteer where he went wrong, and on what he should concentrate next time. As the charioteer becomes more skilled, the captain will explain the type of manoeuvre which the commander will call for, and the kind of service which he, the charioteer, in conjunction with other charioteers, will be fitted to give to the ruler. Once the charioteer has absorbed all that the captain is there to teach, a fresh development takes place. The captain's presence is no longer necessary, and he (the captain) is free to turn his attention to other tasks. The charioteer, having mastered the art of driving a chariot, now has to achieve an 'alignment' with the commander analogous to the 'alignment' which he previously attained with the captain.

D *What is the purpose of human life? Human life can be likened to life at school – the learning of lessons in a school of spiritual development.*

We will begin by noting certain features which all schools have in common. Terms and holidays follow each other in ordered sequence. During the first few terms the pupil has little say about the form or sets in which he or she is put. But as terms pass and progress is made, the pupil, in consultation with the staff, has increasing say about the course to be pursued and the time to be spent on different subjects. At appropriate stages in the course there are examinations to be sat. If these are not passed, they have to be retaken. A point of some importance is to notice the extent to which specialisation takes place. Not even the most brilliant pupil is expected to be, or indeed can be, proficient at everything. Nor for that matter are the staff.

After the start of each holidays an important event occurs – the arrival of the report which reviews progress made during the term just finished. If the term's progress has been satisfactory the subsequent holidays are likely to be a period of mainly enjoyable re-creation and assimilation. If examinations are looming or because of innate keenness, the pupil may, of his/her own freewill, do work which will prove helpful in the forthcoming term. This is then likely to be spent doing more advanced work, maybe in a higher form or set. If, however, the term's progress has been unsatisfactory, the holidays are likely to be marred by having to do work which may well prove uncongenial in order to make good opportunities lost during the preceding term.

Let us now consider what happens during a particular term. The form and sets in which the pupil is placed depend on three main factors. What the pupil has already learnt at the school; the pupil's capacity to learn, as exemplified by past progress; and what the pupil wants to do in the future. Assuming that form and sets have been settled and that term is under way, there are two points which warrant attention. First, that the framework of the pupil's life at school is largely laid down. Classes and sundry other activities take place at appointed times over which he/she has little or no control. Freewill is severely restricted. But where there is little external constraint and the pupil has almost complete freewill is in his/her actions and reactions within the prescribed framework. Is a particular lesson – and not just lessons – something to be enjoyed, to be resented, to be learnt from, or to be slept through? About this – *his/her attitude of mind* – the pupil has complete freedom. And it is this which will determine the term's progress, and what happens subsequently. Second, that it is most unwise for a pupil to judge his or her schoolmates. Is it realised, for example, that John, who is struggling with mathematics, a subject which he dislikes and for which he has no talent, is brilliant at foreign languages? Or that Mary, who may be poor at games, has the making of a first class musician? Only the staff are in a position to make a judgement based on adequate knowledge, and often even they will be hesitant to do so. On leaving school, perhaps after a short spell as prefect, the majority of pupils go into a job or enter institutions of further education. But one or two may join the staff, either at once or after an interval. Every school has a Head who, though not permanent, often remains at the school for a somewhat longer period than the pupils.

In this allegory terms correspond to lives lived in physical incarnation, and holidays to the periods between. The termly report has its parallel in the review/judgement which follows each incarnation. The extent to which man has freewill is a question which has haunted him since he first began to think. And there is still no clear cut answer. At school, as already pointed out, there is comparatively little freedom regarding the actual framework of timetable, classes, games, meals, etc., but a great deal of freedom in respect of the pupil's attitude of mind in relation to what happens within the framework. Perhaps everyday life is not dissimilar. Not a great deal of freedom about what actually happens, but a great deal of freedom as to how we react to what happens – our attitude of mind. Just as at school, may it be this which progressively determines our future, both short and long term? About passing moral judgement on others, suffice it to say that this has been deprecated by all the great religious teachers, *tout comprendre, c'est tout pardonner.*

On a cosmic time scale the school has not perhaps been in existence all that long and is still in process of building up, so that the great majority of pupils are in the second and third forms, and the number in the fifth and sixth forms, the forms in which examinations are taken, is still very very small. Two important questions remain. What is the purpose of the school of life? And who are the staff? To the first question, the answer which suggests itself is 'To educate its pupils to perform whatever parts they are called upon to play in the drama of life with grace, skill, and selfless dedication.' To the second question a possible answer is 'Some of those who have passed through the school, or some comparable school, successfully.' And could it be that the Christ is the Head of the School, responsible to the Lord of the World for the spiritual evolution of the race? And that Jesus is the Teacher responsible to the Christ for the development of the Christian religion?

E   Ω *(omega), the End to which all life moves. The End is an ever expanding and ever deepening consciousness – the Kingdom of Heaven or Nirvana.*

The final picture is of a great mountain peak, the Mount of Illumination, whose lower reaches are swathed in mist and cloud, but whose snowcapped summit sparkles in the sun. Maps exist and there are guides; but there are no chair lifts or cable cars. The only way up is by climbing. Like all great peaks, the Mount of Illumination has many faces and many ridges, and there are numerous ways of ascent. These call for varying degrees of skill, courage, and determination, but none of the ways is easy. From points near the base of the mountain, the view will be restricted, and from points some distance apart what is observed will vary considerably. On any route the view unfolds as greater height is achieved, and what is seen by people on different routes progressively overlaps. When the summit is attained the view is, of course, the same for all. Though the significance of what is seen will be coloured by the route which has been followed.

55

In this allegory the height achieved at any given time symbolises the range of the climber's awareness.

References

1. 1 Thessalonians 5:23
2. Philippians 4:8
3. *The Sayings of the Ancient One*, P. G. Bowen, (Rider & Co., 1935, republished by the Theosophical Publishing House), chap. v
4. *The Path*, vol. IX, Dec. 1894. In a letter to her sister Vera, Madame Blavatsky writes as follows –

    Someone comes and envelopes me as a misty cloud and all at once pushes me out of myself and then I am not 'I' any more – Helena Petrovna Blavatsky – but someone else. Someone strong and powerful, born in a totally different region of the world; and as to myself it is almost as if I were asleep, only lying by not quite conscious – not in my own body but close by, held only by a thread which ties me to it. However, at times I see and hear everything quite clearly; I am perfectly conscious of what my body is saying and doing – or at least its new possessor. I even understand and remember it all so well afterwards I can repeat it and even write down his words . . .

    This illustrates the possibility of overshadowing and, incidentally, throws considerable light on how that remarkable book *The Secret Doctrine* came to be written
5. *The Rays and the Initiations*, Alice A. Bailey, (Lucis Press, 1960), pp. 524 & 695
6. *The Secret Doctrine*, H. P. Blavatsky, (Theosophical Publishing House, Adyar Edition, 1950), vol. 3, p. 161
7. *The Occult Way*, P. G. Bowen, (Occult Book Society, 1938, republished by the Theosophical Publishing House), p. 28
8. Romans 7:19

5: Testing by Experience

In this chapter we shall consider what bearing the experience of mystics, recent developments in psychology and science, and the cumulative evidence of the paranormal, have on the hypothesis and allegories described in the preceding chapter.

Mysticism

Until recently a mystical experience was regarded as something which only happened to a few, and that to be one of the few you had to be a saint! But today, subject to a sufficiently broad definition of mysticism, this view is known to be false. Defining a mystical state of consciousness as one in which normal consciousness is transcended, the painstaking work of Sir Alister Hardy and his 'Religious Experience Research Unit' at Manchester College, Oxford, has shown convincingly that, at some time in their life, one in three or one in four of the population is likely to have a mystical or peak experience.[1] It must not be thought, however, that such experiences are all of the same kind. The situation is rather like asking a group of people whether they are living at home or abroad. And if they say 'abroad', assuming that they are all living in the same country! Mystical or peak experiences vary widely, both in kind and in depth. But many do refer to:
  (a) Transcendence of the world of the five physical senses, and of space and time as normally understood.
  (b) Certainty about the significance and reality of their experience.
  (c) Conviction that love and perfection underlie all that is.
  (d) Unity, at-one-ment.

Moreover, these characteristics are largely independent of the particular religious faith (if any) of the person having the experience. In connection with (d), and the vexed question of – at-one-ment with what? – the following ostensible communication from an advanced soul is significant.

> Too considerable a revelation of God would drive the most spiritual human being mad. The highly gifted mystic or yogi was never in his earthly life-time united with God. Actually, his little spark was blown on so that it became a tiny flame during the occasions he had mystical experiences. Only when the long journey through infinite time has been made, only when the human soul has been fully used for the purposes of Divine Imagination, and this soul is incomparably enriched by the strength of all the other souls in its Group, can it experience Union with Divine Imagination. To be on the level with God one has to become a god, and that full glory is not to be experienced by any human being.[2]

Mystical experience, such as that referred to in the preceding paragraphs, is entirely consistent with the allegory of cells in the human body. That man can, on occasion, be partially and temporarily receptive to the consciousness of a more exalted being is just what would be expected. But, by analogy with the relationship between the cells and organs in a human body and the informing consciousness of that body, it is only reasonable to assume that there is a whole hierarchy of beings who work for, and within the body of, the Lord of the World. To attempt to classify them is pointless because impossible at our present stage of spiritual insight and development. But to think of such beings as God, as some people tend to do, is a dangerous and misleading over-simplification.

An individual's first hand experience is something to which he (or she) has an inalienable right and which can never be taken away. But the *interpretation* of that experience is another matter, and may be open to a number of differing explanations. This applies especially to the *identity* of an exalted being with whom someone feels that he (or she) has been in contact. In touch with an exalted being; yes, indeed. But that particular being? When enquired into further, the reason often amounts to, 'But who else could it be?' Not a convincing proof of identity! The exalted being may be a particular saint or saintly character to whom the person concerned has been especially attracted or in the habit of praying, but it may not. What matters is the contact and the inspiration that has flowed from it.

Psychology

There are, today, many schools of psychology, whose tenets range from those which adhere to an out and out behaviourist concept of man – the belief that eventually everything will be explicable in terms of the purely physical – to those which, while accepting the contribution made by behaviourism, maintain that in itself it is but a pale and often deceptive sign of something far more deeply interfused. In an attempt to coordinate and synthesise the vast amount of studies and research material now available, Dr Assagioli, the founder of psychosynthesis, has 'arrived at a pluridimensional conception of the human personality' which he considers to be 'more inclusive and nearer to reality than previous formulations'.[3] A diagrammatic representation of this conception is reproduced in the figure.

The notes which follow are extracts from, or summaries of, Dr Assagioli's observations.

The Lower Unconscious (1)
This contains the elementary psychological activities which direct the life of the body, the intelligent co-ordination of bodily functions; the fundamental drives and primitive urges; many complexes, charged with intense emotion; dreams and imaginations of an inferior kind; lower, uncontrolled parapsychological processes; various pathological manifestations, such as phobias, obsessions, compulsive urges and paranoid delusions.

59

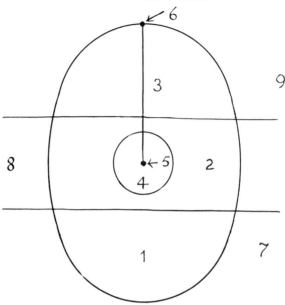

The Middle Unconscious (2)
This is formed of psychological elements similar to those of waking consciousness and easily accessible to it. In this inner region our various experiences are assimilated, and developed before their birth into the light of consciousness.

The Higher Unconscious or Superconscious (3)
From this region we receive our higher intuitions and inspirations – artistic, philosophical or scientific. It is the source of the higher feelings, such as altruistic love; of genius and of the states of contemplation, illumination, and ecstasy. In this realm are latent the higher psychic functions and spiritual energies.

The Field of Consciousness (4)
This term is used to designate that part of our personality of which we are directly aware: the incessant flow of sensations, images, thoughts, feelings, desires, and impulses which we can observe, analyse, and judge.

The Conscious Self or 'I' (5)
This is the point of pure self-awareness, not to be confused with the conscious personality described in the preceding paragraph. The changing contents of our consciousness (the sensations, thoughts, feelings, etc.) are one thing; the 'I', the self, the centre of our consciousness is another.

The Higher Self (6)
The higher self is above, and unaffected by, the flow of the mindstream or by bodily conditions; and the personal conscious self should be considered merely as its reflection, its 'projection' in the field of the personality. This concept is corroborated by 'such philosophers as Kant and Herbart, who make a clear distinction between the empirical ego and the noumenal or real Self.'

The Lower, Middle, and Higher Collective Unconscious (7), (8), (9)
The outer line of the oval of the diagram should be regarded as 'delimiting' but not as dividing. It should be regarded as analogous to the membrane delimiting a cell, which permits a constant and active interchange with the whole body to which the cell belongs. Processes of 'psychological osmosis' are going on all the time, both with other human beings and with the general psychic environment. The latter corresponds to what Jung has called the collective unconscious.

For the writer the most striking features of Dr Assagioli's description of man are the delineation of the conscious self or 'I', and the existence of the higher self. These correspond so well with the charioteer and the captain in the allegory of the chariot. As do also the lower unconscious with the horses and reins, and the higher unconscious with the commander and ruler.

Science

Scene: two people. A philosopher (X), and a pragmatist (Y)

| X. What is mind? | Y. It doesn't matter |
| X. What is matter? | Y. Never mind. |

The branches of science which bear most directly on the questions under discussion are biology and physics. Biology, because of its concern with life. Physics, because of its interest in the nature of matter.

Biology

The belief that everything, including life itself, will ultimately be explicable in terms of physics and chemistry – the mechanistic theory of life in which living organisms are regarded as physico-chemical machines – may still be held by a majority of those working in the biological field, but a growing minority has come to think otherwise. Reasons vary, but the considerations which follow have undoubtedly been a factor.

It is now apparent that chance mutations followed by natural selection cannot, on their own, provide a satisfactory explanation of the evolution of life. For it can be shown unequivocally that the probability that various links in the evolutionary chain have occurred by chance – links such as the formation of complex organic molecules and the existence of specific polymers necessary for the manifestation of life – is utterly remote.[4] The implications of this discovery are far reaching, as indicated by the title of the book edited by the eminent biochemist, E. Lester Smith, *Intelligence Came First*.[5] In addition to these quantitative considerations, it is difficult, when surveying the broad sweep of evolution, to avoid an overall impression of underlying purpose. The molecular biologists claim that the apparent purposiveness of the structure and behaviour of living organisms can be explained in terms of random genetic mutations followed by natural selection. But as Sheldrake points out in *A New Science of Life*,[6] this claim does little to answer the following questions. How do new structures appear which cannot be explained in terms of the growth of structures which are present in the egg at the beginning of development? How is it that if part of a developing system is removed, the system continues to develop in such a way that a more or less normal structure is developed – a phenomenon that happens quite often? How is it that organs are frequently able to replace or restore damaged structure; e.g. plants, and many of the lower animals? And finally, the problem posed by reproduction: how can a detached part of the parent become a new organism, how can a part become a whole? Considerations such as these lead to the conclusion that a living organism has a unity of its own and cannot be understood in terms of the union of its parts, a conclusion voiced among others by the Nobel Laureate, Michael Polanyi.[7]

A further challenge to the mechanistic interpretation of life is provided by recent investigations into the influence of mind on matter. In *The Romeo Error*, Lyall Watson gives some telling examples of this, ending up with his conviction, based on first hand experience, that some of the Philippine healers can produce 'repeatable macroscopic materialisation of living tissue'.[8] That mind can, on occasion, influence matter in this way shows conclusively that mind is primary, matter secondary, and not the other way round. At a recent conference on *Evolution of Consciousness*, Sir John Eccles, another Nobel Laureate, stated that he had arrived at the certainty that mind existed apart from its instrument the brain, though warning the other scientists present that there was formidable opposition to this conclusion![9] Linked with this is the growing interest in the existence and nature of energy fields surrounding the physical body, a subject that was first studied by Professor H. S. Burr of Yale University nearly fifty years ago.[10] About such fields, Lyall Watson, a biologist with exceptionally wide interests, has this to say.

> The assumption of a second system intimately associated with the normal body, does provide answers for all kinds of problems that we have left hanging without solution. The organiser that produces the directional patterns of life and death could be located here. Information acquired by the physical body or the somatic system could be stored as integral parts of this organiser and provide a base for memory and

recall. If such a fellow traveller does exist, I think it is necessary to assume that it does have some physical reality and is not unlocated like some cosmic vapour. To be at all useful as an answer to biological problems, it would need to be so closely associated with the normal somatic system that any change in one would more or less immediately be mirrored in the other.[11]

[Professor] William Teller of Stanford University believes that the evidence we already have is enough to prove that the somatic system is supplemented by at least one other. He calls the combination the 'human ensemble' and suggests that the most reasonable approach yet made to an interpretation of this complex is the yogic philosophy of the seven principles.[12]

The preceding observations are in striking agreement with what is said in Chapter 8 about the etheric field or body of vitality.

Another interesting development in the biological field is the discovery, following the use of increasingly sophisticated apparatus, that 'there is in principle no ultimate gap between living and dead matter . . . and that living organisms can best be described as non-living matter that has become organised in a special and different way.'[13] The extent to which 'inert matter' is in fact intensely 'alive' is a recent discovery of subatomic physics and is referred to in the next section.

Physics

Physics has always been deeply interested in the nature of matter and with discovering the ultimate building blocks of which it was thought to be composed. At the beginning of last century the Newtonian model reigned supreme. This asserted the existence of absolute space and absolute time, that any two bodies were attracted to each other by the *force* of gravity, and that matter was made up of material particles which were small, solid, and indestructible. Such a model implied that the universe resembled a machine whose behaviour was entirely predictable. The first serious crack in what appeared at the time as an unassailable intellectual edifice was due to Faraday and Clerk Maxwell who were responsible for the concept of the electromagnetic *field*. At the turn of the century there were therefore two models – Newton's and Maxwell's. Then came Einstein, whose discoveries showed that though the Newtonian model was valid (i.e. a good approximation) in 'the zone of middle dimensions', our ordinary work-a-day world, it did not hold for the very large or the very small. To investigate these it was necessary to use relativity theory for the very large and quantum theory for the very small. Results followed which were unexpected and far reaching. It was found that mass and energy are no longer independent: mass can be transformed into energy and energy can be changed into mass. In *The Tao of Physics*, Fritjof Capra, a distinguished atomic physicist, puts it like this:

> The creation of material particles from pure energy is certainly the most spectacular effect of relativity theory. All particles can be transmuted into other particles; they can be created from energy and can vanish into energy. Classical concepts like 'elementary particle', 'material substance', or 'isolated object', have lost their meaning; the whole universe appears as a dynamic web of inseparable energy patterns.[14]
> The various models of subatomic physics express again and again that the constituents of matter and the basic phenomena involving them are interconnected, interrelated and interdependent, and they cannot be understood as isolated entities, but only as integrated parts of the whole.[15]

It has been found, too, that space and time are no longer unconnected, and that they are components of a four-dimensional space-time continuum. Space is curved to different degrees and time flows at different rates in different parts of the universe. This leads to the observation that

> [Subatomic] particles must not be pictured as three-dimensional objects, but rather as four-dimensional entities in space-time. They are dynamic patterns which have a space aspect and a time aspect. Their space aspect makes them appear as objects with a certain mass, their time aspect as processes involving the equivalent energy.[16]

And finally,

> [The latest] theory of sub-atomic particles reflects the impossibility of separating the scientific observer from the observed phenomena . . . It implies, ultimately, that the structures and phenomena we observe in nature are nothing but creations of our measuring and categorising mind.[17]

In *The Human Situation*, Macneile Dixon says that 'Science sheds its last year's conclusions as a snake its skin.'[18] Allowing for a little poetic licence, he has a case. For the changes which have occurred in physics during the last hundred years have been immense. And there is no good reason for supposing that during the next hundred years changes will not be just as great. What then can we pick on, which is accepted today – at least by many if not by all – and which is likely to remain essentially unaltered? It seems to the writer that such will probably include the following:

(a) The demise of the mechanistic world view, and of the belief in absolute space and absolute time.
(b) The pre-eminent importance of energy fields.
(c) The universe viewed as 'a harmonious indivisible whole; a network of dynamic relations that include the human observer and his or her consciousness in an essential way.'[19]

Capra in *The Tao of Physics*, and Lawrence LeShan in *The Medium, the Mystic, and the Physicist*[20] and its sequel *Alternate Realities*,[21] have emphasised the remarkable parallel between the experience of mystics, of both East and West, and the findings of atomic physicists during the last fifty years. The similarities and their implications are discussed at length in the books just referred to. The two examples which follow, taken from *The Medium, the Mystic, and the Physicist*, are illustrative and typical.

> There are indeed fundamentally two categories of knowledge – Knowledge by Ideation and Knowledge by Being. All scientific knowledge, whether physical or super-physical, belongs to the first category. Such knowledge is based on the duality of the

observer and observed. In Spiritual perception, however, there is Knowledge by Being – it arises in that state where the duality of the observer and the observed has vanished. This is the very core of direct or what is otherwise called the Mystical experience.[22]

Rohit Mehta, a serious mystic

These two ways of thinking, the way of time and history and the way of eternity and timelessness, are both parts of man's effort to comprehend the world in which he lives. Neither is comprehended in the other nor reducible to it. They are, as we have learned to say in physics, complementary views, each supplementing the other, neither telling the whole story.[23]

J. Robert Oppenheimer, the well known atomic physicist

Although the model suggested in Chapter 4 extends a long way beyond the present findings of biology and physics, it is probably fair to say that the direction in which these sciences are moving is not at variance with the picture portrayed by the model.

The Paranormal

The paranormal covers a vast range of physical and mental happenings which until recently were viewed with the utmost suspicion. This was largely due to proven cases of fraud, especially in relation to the production of physical phenomena, and to the difficulty – in most cases the impossibility – of conducting repeatable experiments under controlled conditions. Of late, however, the climate has undergone a change. Laboratory experiments, conducted with meticulous care, have established beyond any doubt the existence in certain people of unusual mental faculties, such as telepathy and clairvoyance. And the cumulative evidence provided by other happenings is such that assertions of deliberate fraud, unconscious misrepresentation, or mere coincidence, can no longer provide a credible explanation. So the whole subject is now wide open for investigation, though the academic establishment continues to view the subject with a combination of misgiving and distaste!

Those branches of the paranormal which are of most immediate interest are those which involve the influence of mind on matter (p.k. phenomena), and evidence for survival and reincarnation. The most convincing up-to-date account of evidence that mind can, on occasion, influence matter directly is contained in Professor Hasted's *The Metal-Benders*.[24] After reading this book there is little scope for doubting that p.k. phenomena – however disturbing the implications! – can and do occur. And to describe such happenings as disturbing is no exaggeration, because they indicate that mind and matter can no longer be regarded as the wholly independent categories which many have thought them to be.

Evidence relating to the question of survival is vast in quantity but of very uneven quality, and to sift the wheat from the chaff is far from easy. The subject has been surrounded with so much emotion and prejudice that it is difficult to consider the problem with emotional dispassion and intellectual honesty. The main sources of evidence include apparitions, often at or near the moment of death; automatic writing; mediums in trance; and sensitives not in trance. Examples, illustrating the kind of evidence which each of these sources can provide, together with examples of evidence which does not fit neatly into any of these categories, are given in *The Sacred Quest*. After a careful consideration of the evidence – for there is no other way of coming to a responsible decision – what is the outcome? There is no 'cast iron' proof which many look for; so it is a matter of assessing where the balance of probability lies. And this involves a subjective element which varies greatly from one person to another. For reasons explained in *The Sacred Quest* the writer considers that the cumulative evidence for personal survival is now overwhelming and therefore accepts continued existence after physical death as a fact. But when we enquire as to its nature, we enter a much more difficult field. The best account to date of this relatively uncharted territory is probably *Living On* by Paul Beard.[25] This embodies the results of a lifetime's study conducted with a high degree of emotional dispassion and intellectual detachment. What follows is a summary of some of the main points.

After physical death, which is in itself an entirely painless process (not to be confused with a preceding illness which may have been anything but painless), the individual 'wakes up' after a period of unconsciousness analogous to sleep. The world in which he (or of course she) finds himself appears at first to be surprisingly similar to the physical world which has just been left. But soon some striking differences emerge. The most important is that by concentrated thought he can mould, if not create, his surroundings. This remarkable characteristic provides the key to understanding the 'next world', i.e. the band of consciousness to which we respond immediately after physical death. *It is a thought created world.* A world created by the thoughts of those who have been there in the past but are there no longer, modified by the thoughts of those who are there now. (A valid description of the artifacts of the world in which we live now, subject to 'thoughts' being replaced by 'actions'.) But in this world, there are many different 'levels'. These include 'levels' on which conditions are relatively pleasant, the 'Summer Land' of mediumistic communications, but there are also 'levels' on which conditions are anything but pleasant, and which Beard calls the 'Winter Land'. The determining factor is a person's innermost thoughts and feelings. If a person's attitude of mind is coarse, hard, and unloving, so will be his surroundings. If his attitude is refined, gentle, and loving, his surroundings will reflect these qualities. Hence such phrases (from ostensible communications) as 'each goes to his own place', and 'so I found my location'.

To anyone meeting these ideas for the first time they may seem very strange. But before what has been outlined is dismissed as fantasy, let us reflect for a moment on the nature of the physical world with which we are all so familiar and which we take so much for granted. On ultimate analysis it is an immensely complex energy pattern in space that is otherwise assumed to be empty. But this is a far cry from the table at which I am writing or the chair on which I am sitting. What is so remarkable – though not regarded as remarkable because it is happening all the time – is the capacity of the human mind to interpret energy patterns as tables and chairs replete with secondary qualities such as colour, hardness and smell. We fail to realise, or if we realise we overlook, the extent to which we live here and now in a thought created world. With this in mind, is hypothesising the existence of different energy patterns which our minds can interpret in a different way really so extraordinary? Would not a fairer appraisal of the position be surprise if it were not so?

For the sake of convenience the 'next world' – the world in which everyone 'wakes up' after undergoing physical death – will be referred to as the 'astral world' (a world in which everything has a certain self-luminosity and so has led to the use of the word 'astral'). Because it is thought created, the astral world is sometimes referred to as a world of illusion. In one sense it is, but it appears completely objective, and therefore real, to those who inhabit it. The astral world being 'nearest' to the material world of the five physical senses, it follows that in so far as communication with someone who has died is possible at all, it is easier, and therefore most likely to occur, when the departed one is in this world. There seems little doubt that the great majority of mediumistic communications are from this region. The fact that it is a world created by the thoughts of those who have recently, or relatively recently, been alive on earth explains why so many of the communications from the other side are lacking in wisdom and insight. But in the great beyond, life is no more static than it is on earth. When those in the 'Winter Land' realise their gloomy condition and seek for light, light is forthcoming in the form of help, and a change to less restrictive conditions becomes possible. And those in the 'Summer Land'? For them life is pleasant. The realisation of one's personal desires brings satisfaction – for a time. But gradually the satisfaction begins to pall. Life is too easy. Something is lacking. Moreover, complacency is shaken in another way, for the individual finds that, though he is happy with his companions, certain of them disappear! They have 'gone on'; they have realised that their life now needs to be lived more strenuously. When this stage is reached, realisation starts to dawn about the true nature of the astral world, and a feeling that the time has come to embark on the next stage of life's journey into the beyond.

This next stage is the judgement: a detailed review of the life just lived, carried out in the presence of, and with the help of a teacher. In *Living On* Paul Beard describes it thus:

> The point is that in some manner the traveller is shown every single event in his life as it really was and not as he thought it had been. The record is made straight wherever he misunderstood it. But there is more: besides his own deeds and the thoughts and feelings connected with them, he is also now obliged actually to experience within himself the thoughts and feelings, the pains and pleasures which his actions caused in the lives of other people; exactly what he caused them to feel he, in turn, feels in himself now. This is a surprising and very disconcerting event.[26]

The significance of this experience can scarcely be overemphasised, both for the individual and generally. The individual realises for perhaps the first time, not what he thinks himself to be, but what he really is – for most people a rather disturbing discovery. There is no question of inflicted punishment. The sole punishment is to observe oneself as one really is, and to see and experience what one has done, or maybe not done, for others in the course of the life just lived. As the judgement proceeds, purgation occurs, and the individual will wish to make amends (in so far as this is possible) for 'all those things which he ought to have done, and all those things which he ought not to have done'. Where possible and appropriate he will give help to those on earth either telepathically or when they are asleep. He will also take advantage of the opportunity to study the spiritual laws and principles which provide the framework for the development of life, in particular human life, on this planet. The 'level' on which the individual is now conscious is still within the astral world, but the environment, though a mental creation, is of a much more permanent character.

Before considering what happens next, let us note the change which has taken place since physical death. There has been a gradual withdrawal of consciousness from preoccupation with the personal self, the personality, to concern for the well-being of the group. The focus of consciousness has been gradually shifting from the personal to the impersonal, from the personality to the soul or deep centre, from eros to agape.

In the East the concept of sheaths and the consciousness associated with a particular sheath is not unfamiliar. Physical sensing made possible by the physical sheath (the physical body), emotional feeling dependent on the emotional sheath, and so on. In the West such thinking is unfamiliar, and even the idea that human consciousness can persist without a physical body is, for many, unacceptable. This is a pity, because the next stage of the journey involves casting off the emotional sheath in an analogous manner to that in which the physical sheath (the physical body) was discarded. This casting off, sometimes referred to as the second death, is followed by a growing consciousness of the heaven world, in Christian terms the Kingdom of Heaven. The persona or mask has been removed; the personality, with all its once treasured desires and wants has been left behind. The individuality remains.

It will be felt by many that this means the giving up, the sacrifice, of everything that makes life worth while. But is this really so? For life can be likened to a ladder, and the act of living to the process of climbing this ladder. The only security is when standing still on a step. In the process of moving from one step to a higher one this is lacking. The security of standing on the lower step has been sacrificed, and what will be achieved by mounting the higher step has not yet been realised. Reflection shows that this is indeed a picture of human life, a periodical movement from one step to a higher one with the associated sacrifice of what is known, and the inevitable uncertainty about what is to be experienced.

The following is an extract from a noteworthy chapter in *Living On*, and refers to the enhanced consciousness of the heaven world. It is part of a remarkable communication from 'the other side'.

There are times when we have to be set apart to undergo a retreat, in order to understand more of our development . . . During this retreat, I was shown not only my earth life, but the whole course of my evolution . . . Once you have conquered and risen above the small self, you can go through the test . . . you can learn so much from it and yet feel no pain, because you see how each mistake was turned to your advantage in spite of yourself, by the light of the Divinity within you working as far as you would allow it to do so.

You are able to see the line of gold which has persisted through everything, and you think only of that. You store in your aura all the lessons you think will be helpful to you in future intercourse with other people, or in any work that you may be given to do . . .

I saw that through the whole course of my evolution, *comparison* was the attitude of mind which had led to my undoing again and again, or had weakened the good of the work I was able to do. I do ask you, never allow yourself to compare: never think to yourself, 'why was I given this and another given that, what was the difference?' If you could see, you would probably realise that there was no difference underneath the surface, it was simply a case of adjusting the gift to fit in with your evolution . . . the larger self knows the reality behind, it is only the small personal self, the mind, which makes you compare . . .

I saw that often I could have developed several gifts which seemed to me easier to use and better suited to the work that I was doing, than the one I had developed; but the Divinity within . . . saw that it was for my good to develop a gift which might appear to me inferior. I even saw that sometimes, when I had developed a gift and was in danger of being proud of my

success and taking too much to myself, the gift was veiled over
. . .

It was interesting to see the same temptation being met round
after round: and to see that if I had conquered in one round, the
temptation was not put so directly in my way in the next round,
or it took a more subtle form, and I therefore may have
succumbed to it. If I did succumb, I found that in the following
round temptation assailed me on every side, and I had to
right it almost to save my life, therefore I was forced to
overcome it – a very drastic and effectual way of education. I
saw that clearly, throughout my evolution, but I also saw that I
was never faced with temptation in that very severe manner
until I had come to a certain understanding of the Power that
was in me and so knew that within me I possessed the strength
to overcome, if I chose . . . I could see how I have kept the same
attitude of mind right through my evolution, beginning with
comparison which always feeds the smaller self and usually
strengthens self-will.[27]

Paul Beard continues:

There comes to the pilgrim also a blueprint of the new life he
must undergo on earth. He studies the next part of the road
along which he must travel. This blueprint will not, of course,
be punitive, though it will include much that is regenerative in
purpose . . . In these past lives many significant episodes have
been shared by other beings whom the pilgrim now discovers to
be his intimate and long-term companions. Over many years
and many lives he has shared travails and triumphs with them.
In a deep sense they are his brothers and sisters, his companions
of the spirit, and will always remain so. His task is no longer one
for which he is solely responsible; as the horizons lift he sees
that it is really part of a grander task, a group task shared
between him and these others.[28]

There is now at-one-ment with what has been variously
referred to as the higher self, soul, or deep centre. As Albert
Pauchard says:

First I saw Albert Pauchard . . . just as if he were outside me
. . . I realised that the *I* who was observing thus was not 'Albert
Pauchard'.

74

At that instant I gradually recognised *who* I was. I did not see this *real I*, but realised it by an inner warmth which kept on intensifying and increasing in light . . .

I understood then that our 'personality' is only the 'shadow' of our *I*. A 'shadow' which always moves towards perfection – through the lives on earth and the lives in heaven – and which forms itself according to the outline of the one who had given it existence. The outline of the real *I*.[29]

To the surprise of some, and perhaps of many, the idea of reincarnation has arisen from considering the evidence for survival. The task now is to see what (if any) other evidence exists which has a direct bearing on the concept of reincarnation. Though there is nothing which constitutes proof, a survey of the field shows that cumulative evidence is building up to a case of formidable proportions. The empirical evidence is of two main kinds. 'Far memory' which is natural, i.e., innate ('far memory' is the term used to describe the memory of an ostensible previous existence); and 'far memory' which is induced by hypnotism. To have value as evidence, the 'far memory' must be of happenings which are unknown to anyone present, thus ruling out telepathy, but which can subsequently be verified. Such evidence is of three sorts. First, individuals. Cases of this sort have been investigated by Professor Ian Stevenson with great thoroughness and the results published in a number of books and articles, notably *Twenty Cases Suggestive of Reincarnation*[30] and *Cases of the Reincarnation Type* – Vol. 1, 'Ten Cases in India' and Vol. 2, 'Ten Cases in Sri Lanka'.[31] The care with which the evidence has been sifted is impressive, and bearing in mind the number of individuals examined, the case for postulating some sort of reincarnationist hypothesis becomes very strong. Second, groups of individuals who have 'far memories' which are interlocking, i.e. the 'far memories' appear to be of the same place or district and at the same time in history. A most striking example of this is the group of individuals who were ostensibly Cathars in the 13th century and who are the subject of several books by Dr Arthur Guirdham, notably *The Cathars and Reincarnation*[32] and *We are One Another*.[33] The interlocking is of such an extensive nature that super-ESP, as some people have suggested, seems a *very* far fetched explanation. Third, the evidence provided by someone who seems to have an almost complete memory of an earlier life, as distinct from a memory of particular episodes. An example of this is *Second Time Round* by E. W. Ryall,[34] about which Professor Stevenson says in his introduction to the book, 'This brings me to say therefore, that, as of now, I believe it best interpreted as an instance of reincarnation. In other words, I think it most probable that he has memories of a real previous life and that he is indeed John Fletcher reborn, as he believes himself to be.'

The other kind of empirical evidence – 'far memory' induced by hypnotism – is difficult to evaluate with our present knowledge (or, more precisely, lack of knowledge) of hypnotism. The most striking example is provided by the 'readings' made by Edgar Cayce, and described by Gina Cerminara in *Many Mansions*.[35] Striking, too, are the experiments conducted by Dr Helen Wambach and described in her book *Life before Life*[36] and the cases described in *Many Lifetimes* by Joan Grant and Denys Kelsey.[37] But the data from these sources are remarkable and thought provoking rather than evidential, as inevitably so little of what is 'remembered' is capable of being substantiated.

Evidence of a quite different kind is provided by a book such as *The Wheel of Rebirth* by H. K. Challoner.[38] With the aid of a Teacher, the author, through dreams, automatic writing and in other ways, was able to recall and to relive vital episodes in previous lives. Each chapter in the book is devoted to a life, and at the end of each chapter are the Teacher's comments on the life in question. Herein lies the value of the book. About the end of an utterly disastrous life in Greece, the Teacher comments: 'You did not die by your own hand as you imagined; you had done that in several previous incarnations and the futility of such an action had remained part of your mental equipment for all time. On the contrary, those years although apparently so horrible and degraded were the most fruitful of all. For, admitting failure, you sought at last to understand *where* you had failed. You no longer made excuses, you no longer blamed everything but yourself. Free at last of self-deception, you repented; but it was the real repentance. You did not alter your way of living – it was too late; but driven down among the dregs of humanity, you developed understanding, love, and sympathy for your fellow sufferers. Although you knew it not, this experience was a great act of spiritual growth.' The aims and values of a Teacher – one who is preeminently concerned with the spiritual development of individuals and of the race – tend to be somewhat different from the aims and values of the contemporary world!

Concluding this review of the evidence for reincarnation, it is pertinent to point out that it is a fundamental belief of two of the world's great religions – Hinduism and Buddhism; that many eminent Westerners have embraced it – see, for example, *Reincarnation in World Thought* by Joseph Head and S. L. Cranston;[39] and that it could perhaps throw some light on the appalling ethical problem posed by the glaring inequalities attendant on the circumstances of human birth.

The effect of the preceding survey of the paranormal is to give weighty and unambiguous support to the concepts of the soul or deep centre, and of reincarnation. Both of these concepts endorse the hypothesis and allegories suggested in Chapter 4.

But if this planet can be likened to a school – a school whose purpose is none other than to foster the spiritual development of the human race – what of the staff? Are there Teachers? And if so, where and what do they teach? These very important questions are considered in the next chapter.

References

1. *Reports of ecstatic, paranormal or religious experience in Great Britain and the United States*, David Hay and Ann Morley, (Religious Experience Research Unit, Manchester College, Oxford, 1977)
2. *Watcher on the Hills*, Raynor C. Johnson, (Hodder and Stoughton Ltd., 1959), p. 105
3. *Psychosynthesis*, Roberto Assagioli, (Hobbs, Dorman and Co. Inc. New York, 1965), p. 17
4. See *Universe with Man in Mind*, Glen Schaefer, (Translational Press, 1982)
5. *Intelligence Came First*, edited by E. Lester-Smith, (The Theosophical Publishing House, 1975)
6. *A New Science of Life*, Rupert Sheldrake, (Blond and Briggs, 1981), Chap. 1
7. Quoted in ref. 4, p. 12
8. *The Romeo Error*, Lyall Watson, (Hodder and Stoughton, 1974), p. 223
9. See *Wrekin Trust News*, Spring 1982
10. *Blueprint for Immortality*, H. S. Burr, (Neville Spearman, 1972)
11. Ref. 8, p. 112
12. *Ibid.* p. 165
13. *Ibid.* p. 20
14. *The Tao of Physics*, Fritjof Capra, (Fontana, 1971), p. 82
15. *Ibid.* p. 134
16. *Ibid.* p. 213
17. *Ibid.* p. 292
18. *The Human Situation*, W. Macneile Dixon, (Edward Arnold & Co., 1946), p. 56. (First published 1937)
19. *The Turning Point*, Fritjof Capra, (Wildwood House, 1982), p. 32
20. *The Medium, the Mystic, and the Physicist*, Lawrence Le Shan, (Turnstone Press, 1974)
21. *Alternate Realities*, Lawrence Le Shan, (Sheldon Press, 1976)
22. Ref. 20, p. 53
23. *Ibid.* p. 64
24. *The Metal-Benders*, J. B. Hasted, (Routledge & Kegan Paul, 1981)
25. *Living On*, Paul Beard, (George Allen & Unwin, 1980)

26. *Ibid.* p. 99
27. *Ibid.* p. 133
28. *Ibid.* pp. 133, 135
29. *Ibid.* p. 136
30. *Twenty Cases Suggestive of Reincarnation*, Ian Stevenson, (American Society for Psychical Research. First published 1966)
31. *Cases of the Reincarnation Type*, Ian Stevenson. Vol. 1, 'Ten Cases in India' (1975). Vol. 2, 'Ten Cases in Sri Lanka' (1976), (University of Virginia, U.S.A.)
32. *The Cathars and Reincarnation*, Arthur Guirdham, (Neville Spearman, 1970)
33. *We are One Another*, Arthur Guirdham, (Neville Spearman, 1974)
34. *Second Time Round*, E. W. Ryall, (Neville Spearman, 1974)
35. *Many Mansions*, Gina Cerminara, (Neville Spearman, 1974)
36. *Life before Life*, Helen Wambach, (Bantam Books, 1979)
37. *Many Lifetimes*, Joan Grant and Denys Kelsey, (Corgi Books, 1976. First published, 1969)
38. *The Wheel of Rebirth*, H. K. Challoner, (The Theosophical Publishing House, 1969. First published by Rider & Co. 1935)
39. *Reincarnation in World Thought*, Joseph Head and S. L. Cranston, (Julian Press, Inc. New York, 1967)

6: Extracts from Talks by a Teacher

Are there Teachers? This question was referred to in *The Sacred Quest*, where it was pointed out that, although there is no evidence which would constitute proof, the weight of cumulative evidence drawn from many different quarters is highly significant. To the obvious question, 'Why, if such Teachers exist, do they not come into the open and declare themselves', the answer must surely be that 'to do so would make impossible the work which they are here to do.' Such work is primarily concerned, not with helping particular individuals to solve their personal problems – unless, perhaps, by so doing the individuals concerned can become of direct use to the Teacher – but with furthering the spiritual development of the race. One of the ways by which this is done is by communicating ideas to certain persons who are likely to be receptive and capable of acting on the ideas when apprehended. Communication is often by telepathy, either directly with the person or persons concerned or indirectly through a telepathic communicator. For those who are doubtful whether there is such a thing as telepathy the last sentence must seem fantastic. But first hand experience of such a faculty (see Chapter X of *The Sacred Quest*) replaces fantasy by fact!

If, as is now being suggested, Teachers exist – some in, and some out of, physical incarnation – and teach individuals or small groups through the medium of telepathic communication, what do they teach? In particular, what, if anything, do they have to say about the three questions asked in Chapter 2?

Over a number of years the writer has been privileged to see transcripts of some of the communications received by two small groups, one in this country the other overseas, and much of this chapter consists of relevant extracts from these transcripts. To the question 'How do you know that the transcripts are what they purport to be?', the answer can only be, 'By what they contain.' If what is said rings true and good to you, then its acceptance, at least provisionally, is only sensible. If, however, it does not, so be it; what is said should be disregarded. But in coming to a decision, there must always be borne in mind the risk of distortion. Not only has the idea being communicated to be perfectly formed, prior to transmission, but, when received, it has to be 'interpreted', a process which is limited by what is available in the receiver's mind. No channel is perfect.

Although deciding what weight to give to teaching from an unknown source is essentially a personal matter, there are certain criteria which such teaching must satisfy if it is to be taken seriously. In the opinion of the writer important criteria are

(a) The presence of an astringent element, and a total absence of sentimentality. (So much of today's teaching from unspecified sources consists of platitudes laced with sentimentality.)

(b) Loving concern for the well-being of the whole, starting with the group.

(c) Complete respect for man's freewill.

(d) A total absence of anything which exalts the lower self or personality.

Though these four criteria are *necessary* they are not, of course, *sufficient* to ensure that the communicated teaching comes from an inspired source.

Extracts

Teachers – about Themselves

February 1974

We have all come through the same evolution in which you are now participating. We have suffered, we have learned, we

81

have fallen by the wayside. We are still learning our lessons. Therefore we understand, we know your difficulties. We know and we are sad as we watch the turmoil and the strife. But we know the plan and we are at peace with the plan, for we see farther than you, we see the result. You are struggling up the hill. We stand at the top and know that you will reach us. That is the difference.

November 1974

There are many many planes of life. We may be on a plane some distance beyond yours, but there are planes beyond ours, far far beyond ours, of which we know very little. We know about as much of those planes as you know of ours. There are many planes, not one, hidden, as your Church tries to tell you.

The Present World Crisis

September 1975

There is in the future to be such turmoil and upheaval that nearly all the things that people have regarded as sacred, sacrosanct, and stable will be put through the refining fire of suffering, and much will be destroyed permanently. But truth is not destroyed; truth goes on. That is why you must not worry so much about the outer form as the inner spiritual essence.

The most important thing at the moment is that people should be shown spiritual vision – that the ultimate purpose of life, the ultimate meaning of community, the ultimate understanding of a group, should be seen as the raising of man from the personal, through the psychical, to the spiritual. When this vision can be confided and given to new generations, their lives will be transformed. But it will not be easy.

September 1976

Mankind has reached a point where it must turn back towards the Centre from which it has wandered. There is no other way. The Christ power which is the great over-shadowing power of the spirit can so encircle this planet that it can hold back the tide of evil that has arisen from the past. Let us realise that every soul, every group, every community, has not only a duty, more indeed than any duty, to hold forth the light that peace may be established, that the light may so penetrate these forces of evil that they be driven back from whence they came.

This is an old, an ancient power that threatened the planet before so that the world was submerged in flood. Yet the power was drawn together and creation marched on. If this world cannot be brought together in harmony much of it will be destroyed – not by water, but by fire. We realise the fear and yet we also see the passive lack of action because so much of mankind is sunk in the glamour of worldly affairs.

We know of all that is happening. We know of the terror and racial troubles, we know of the famine which is beginning because mankind has maltreated its own earth, we know of the building up of great armaments of destruction. We know. But man has free will and is allowed to go his own way – up to a point. Now that point is nearly reached.

In the great galaxy of planets this has happened before many times; and they are left as dead planets, planets without life yet where life has been. Let not this happen to this most beautiful planet of earth. Pray that it may become the garden it was meant to be, and was created as such. For man has forgotten that all is of the spirit, every atom, all is one. Only when man is in harmony and love with his fellow man will the lion lie down with the lamb. Only when he ceases to take with greed from the animals who serve him, and from the soil on which he lives – only when he has learned that will he know how to live. That is the beginning of the New Age which should come upon this earth and open up the light of the spirit. But only if the majority of mankind turn towards the Centre as prodigal sons back to the Father.

November 1976

You cannot turn people back, you cannot make them return. But you can do much to influence the climate of men's minds and thought, to show them in a gentle way the cause and effect which has brought them at this moment to supreme danger.

The Church has taught, religions have taught, but they have failed. Man has to find himself by his own thought, by his own sufferings, his own realisations. He will have to say 'I will arise and go to my Father'.

December 1976

The earth itself is in trauma for man has debilitated the soil and has ruined much of the natural creation. The soul of this world is in a tremendous state of sorrow, and will turn against those who have so used her for their own advancement.

*　　*　　*

One of the first principles that will have to be taught to all mankind and will not be easy is to overcome the fear and terror of death. For only when mankind realises that death is but a change into a higher consciousness, a deeper understanding of a thought world, only then will wars and fighting and violence cease on this planet. This is the key note of this next age, and now is a great opportunity to send forth the truth, to change the climate of opinion, to teach man about the next stage of a journey which, did he but know it, has never ceased.

February 1977

The greatest drawback to progress in your world is the half-truth. This has become a danger that is not noticed because it is becoming so prevalent. Half-truths spoken by men who are in places of power and influence; half-truths printed in your newspapers, your books; half-truths spoken by men who have no intention of speaking the truth, but who are cloaking their words that they may be taken in two ways. This is one of the greatest dangers in your civilisation today. These half-truths are spoken by men who should be men of integrity. And they are half-lies because behind them the very men and women who utter them have no intention of fulfilling what they say. They cloak their ideas and their thoughts in glamorous webs which people do not realise is a manifestation of double talk.

When you have found what is authentic truth to your mind and your soul, speak it and then live it. There is in the world today this speaking one way and living another. This brings disaster. All these half-truths are building up into a great and dreadful holocaust. Learn to live this truth – for there will be no other way of living and thinking when you leave the physical body. You will not then be able to think in half-truths, for truth will show, will be made manifest.

October 1977

You in your Western world are living in a plane of being which denounces the divine laws which were given through the Hebrew prophets, and which were fulfilled and taught and lifted into grace by the Master of all the Masters, the Christ. The world

84

has become decadent and the laws of God are flouted. The natural law of procreation for the continuance of the species has been degraded into licence by evil and greedy man. The divine laws are disobeyed. The natural laws are ignored at man's peril. Mankind has given its obedience to mammon, and has elevated it to its gods of money and power above all else. This has happened and has recurred time and time again. Until man realises that he is a soul, and is therefore a unit of the divine source of all creation, these periods of degradation will recur.

It is the few who by their own efforts, by their spiritual adhesion to the power of God's will, help to save the world from chaos. If you look back into the long history of mankind, it has been always the few, those precious few, who in times of degradation have raised the standard again. It is because their ceiling of thought lies beyond matter, and they know themselves as souls, as units of the divine power. They are the leaven, they are the precious few to whom the world must look for the coming of light and peace.

November 1978

We do not need to tell you that your planet is on the verge of anarchy, violence and destruction. Peace and destruction are balanced on either side of a tightrope. This is war between good and evil which may go on for some considerable time. The Hierarchy [the inner Government of the world] is poised to send out peace and light for the saving of this beautiful planet. We accept gladly all help that can come from your world. We are also working with the higher planes of the spirit world, the next world in your consciousness. They, too, can understand the seriousness of a break – not an ending – but a break in the evolution that has been planned for this planet.

We see the plan going forth, and we shall continue to see the plan going forth. But the power on earth of evil, of wrong thinking, of fear, of violence, of greed, of anarchy, is very strong.

March 1979

We know that your world is in dire trouble. It is the reaping of what has been sown. It has happened many times before. There is one essential point which has not been understood, accepted, or realised by the human race. And until that point is

85

understood the same cycle will continue. It is that man is a spiritual being, not just a physical body. It is because mankind has not realised this that the same troubles have come over and over again, and return and return. It is because most have not realised this that they grasp all they can get during the short period of their lives – greed for money and greed for power. They have not realised that as spiritual beings they have all that they need *within them* if only it was developed. The spirit is in all men, and was part of the teaching of Jesus.

May 1979

Not until there is quietness, stability, peace and concord – not until there is that – will this country [U.K.] go forward towards its destiny. The destiny is there. We see it. It is for you, all of you, to help bring it to fulfilment.

It needs a great conflagration. But if the conflagration is not on the spiritual side, it will be on the other side. There is no halfway house. The choice is upwards, or outwards into the darkness. We speak as we feel. We speak as we know. This is a most important moment in the history of your country. To bring light into your land, and then to send light forth into other lands that they may gain from seeing what is happening here.

Talk not of coming trouble between one side and another. But hold within you this power of the spirit. It will bring stability, harmony, concord and peace. It will open men's minds, for they are hungry and know it not. They are hungry for the light. They are hungry for peace. They are hungry for the way of the spirit. They are becoming tired and frightened of the way of the flesh, the way of the world. This is the moment when the change should be coming.

God is not mocked. The Plan is there. But it needs cooperation. Let it become the goodwill, the kindliness, the understanding, that has been forgotten. Let it become light in a dark place. There have been these moments of tension before. There have been times when worlds have crumbled because it was impossible to go on. Let not this happen again. Bring not upon yourselves the dissolution, the destruction of this world. The Plan is there. Let love and light, peace and understanding, strength of thought and positive goodwill, bring forth a world in which the spirit rises, in which man and man are brothers.

Ireland

What is happening in Ireland is symptomatic of a condition prevailing in the world at this time. The cause is the rigidity which has for hundreds of years characterised religion. Until a new attitude is taken up by all religions, and expansion synthesises them, the bigotry, self-acclaim, dominance, narrowness and refusal to progress will result in war, wastage and wanton destruction of life.

Foreseeing the Future

August 1977

Not even we, as Teachers, are able to know *if* that which is predicted will come to pass; but we are able to estimate the practical considerations leading to certain results.

October 1978

We are not certain of the future. It may be as we see it and as we long for it to be. But it is the will of God, the will of the great Creator, to give all free will. Therefore his design, his purpose, may be blocked by the selfishness of the people to whom he has given free will. On the other hand, the purpose that is in the mind of the Creator will go forward, whatever happens. You are bound by time. We look ahead to where there is no time. What you may expect in the course of another hundred years may not occur within another thousand. But the purpose and design of evolution will not be changed.

The New Age

October 1976

There is a feeling that if certain people proclaim the New Age coming and speak ecstatically about energies and powers and tongues of ecstasy, these in themselves will produce a transformation in the person. Nothing could be further from the truth. If these powers do come to unformed people, they can cause disintegration as easily as synthesis. If you are to become independent, responsible people, you have to do the work yourself. You cannot expect something from above to take over and do it for you. All that will, in fact, be done is to strengthen you for your own work, so that you will have the supreme joy of becoming fuller people – real persons. But you have to do the work. If your body is unhealthy (due to an undisciplined life style), or if your mind is perverted and unclean, or if your emotions are awry and self-centred, any power that you may get will cause further disintegration of your personality and disintegration of the world around you as well.

July 1979

We are now in that very potent time when much has to be destroyed. All the weeds that have grown up round that sacred tree, planted by the Initiate Jesus, have to be cut down and burned, so that the Tree of Life, the power which is within each soul, begins to flower. It is in these coming months and years, the end of this century, when the cutting down and the burning of the wrong thoughts and ideas in men must be accomplished. That is one of the instances of the time of the latter days. In our understanding, latter days does not mean the end of the world, your world, but the burning away of the dross that has been allowed through men's ignorance to choke the Tree of Life. They will be difficult years. But we are hopeful for we see the different trends and the upliftment of men's minds. The entrance into the New Age may take two or three hundred years; it will not happen overnight.

The Soul

The soul is the link between spirit and matter. It is the Christ principle in man. It is the intervening link between the Creator and his creation – man. It is through the soul that the spirit is apprehended. It is the most important part of man here on earth, and is the link which is all important between the personality and the spirit.

The soul has three attributes. Past memory; present knowledge; and a sense of purpose.

First memory. The soul is the storehouse of memory. During its spells in incarnation, every experience whether good or evil, of progress or of failure, is remembered. So too are good deeds and bad deeds, fulfilments and non-fulfilments. But it is the soul which remembers, not the personality. [Here defined as comprising physical body, emotional nature, and discursive intellect.] Sometimes the soul lets forth a portion of its knowledge, and the personality draws into itself that knowledge This is rare in people with little development, but for those who have learned to meditate, to still the busy conscious mind and listen, the soul begins to open, and a channel is formed between soul and personality. Memories may then flood into the personality. But when this happens it is for a purpose. The soul may wish the personality to face up to the unpleasant realities of a particular situation, or to acquire deeper understanding, or to receive greater inspiration and intuition. For most of what passes for inspiration and intuition is recalling from the soul knowledge learned in some previous incarnation. Nothing is lost in any venture into incarnation. The soul remembers and recalls at will. It is the personality that draws the blind and says 'I do not want to know.'

Next, present knowledge. For the soul has knowledge of a kind which the personality, confined to matter and to earthly conditions, has not got. When the personality is aligned with the soul, greater knowledge becomes available to the personality. For the soul is fully conversant with the life plan of the personality which it inhabits, with what the personality came to do. The soul is not apart from the personality, though of this the personality is unaware. It therefore behoves the personality to strive to learn from the soul, and to allow the soul to control, to guide, to oversee the personality. The Ajna chakra, the centre between the eyebrows, is the seat of the soul, and it is through that centre that the personality receives inspiration and intuition.

So much that is written is written from the intellect. The words are dead words, uninspired, and fail to draw forth from the reader that raising of the consciousness into another realm that flows from the union of soul and personality. This is why poets, perhaps without realising the source of their inspiration, are able to produce poems which appeal to the heart, mind, and soul of their readers. Such is inspiration, such is intuition. When, later, the personality and soul are at one, the spirit can come flooding in. But it is only via the soul that the spirit can flood into the personality.

Finally, a sense of purpose. The soul remembers the past and is in touch with the future. It is the instrument of purpose. The soul knows the pathway you should tread, the work you should

89

do, and the progress you are here to make. It knows where your difficulties lie, and where are your opportunities. Jesus said 'Take no thought for the morrow.' If you are working with the soul, you need truly take no thought for the material morrow, for the morrow will be brought into the pattern and purpose for which the soul has incarnated. If the personality fails to make contact with the soul, it will skid off the path and lose its way. The personality may turn aside and a great opportunity could be lost. The soul knows the plan for your life, and wants you to follow the purpose which is the will of God, the will of the Creator, for you. Is it not written that the hairs of your head are numbered? How much more then must the soul know of the plan and purpose of your lives?

Your objective now is to become a soul-infused personality; eventually it will be to become a spirit-infused soul.

A soul-infused personality seeks not its own good; it is not interested in itself any more. It has no fear, it is not concerned about the opinions of anyone else. It is full of compassion and love. It is full of simplicity – that simplicity which only the very great saints know when their love flows out to all created things, that simplicity which is the heart of true love and is the nature of the soul when guided by the spirit of Christ within it. In a personality which is infused with the soul every aspect of the personality is changed. The body is changed and the mind is changed, and all work to the glory of God. This leads to joy, the joy that not only is not overcome by outer circumstances, but overcomes the outer circumstances and converts them into a new blessing.

Service

True service is undertaken with no thought of success, no idea of importance, self-glory or reward in any form whatever. The disciple can undertake one work as easily as another, finding joy only in the task. He does not seek rewards but work; he does not identify with the work but with the need; he is not impelled by his reaction to the need but by his ability to fulfil that need through service; and he is not glamoured by a sentimental attitude to service. He knows only what he can do and he goes about doing it silently and to the best of his ability.

Learn that naught matters in the infinitude of time and space excepting that which will aid the Lord of the World in His purpose.

The Distant View

When the beauty of art embraces teaching, then will the healing power of joy be released and the Christ will be an accepted Teacher of all humanity. When sharing dominates the principles of economy, then will the healing power of peace be spread abroad and the Christ will be the accepted consciousness of all humanity. When science is applied under the law of love, then will the Christ instil his truth into the race of men. And when money and health and education are correctly handled without selfishness and for the good of the whole, then will unity and inclusiveness, tolerance and service, be the keynote of living.

Some Questions Put to the Teachers

The concept of reincarnation is becoming more widespread. But with it is often associated the idea that it is only a few who return: the specially good, or the specially bad, or those who for some special reason want to come back. This, however, is not consistent with the teaching that reincarnation is a spiritual law and applies until the attainment of a certain level of spiritual development. Is it right to consider reincarnation as a spiritual law?

Quite right. Why should there be discrimination when all souls have the same chance? Why should some be chosen to come back and others left to wait? Why should only the very good or the very bad as you call them come back? What about those in between? They are still the sheep; they are still of the flock, are they not? It is the law of return and rise, of return and learn and overcome. But there is no definite force used to send a soul back into incarnation. That soul must make the decision in his own way and in his own time. He must realise his own faults and what he could, perhaps, overcome. But the decision must be his. He will, of course, be advised and guided by the greater souls who have passed through these trials, but he will never be forced.

91

If people realised what their thinking and doing will bring upon them as karma in future lives, they would be much more careful, would they not? Surely therefore the doctrine of reincarnation which has been thrown out by the Christian Church should be brought back to give people an insight into why they are here.

What meaning is to be attached to the statement 'divine grace transcends the law of karma'?

Every individual is a progressive atom of consciousness. At this stage of evolution most of the human race are aware on only one level of consciousness, that of the material level. And history has shown that the development of this level of awareness has taken thousands, even millions, of your earth years. Evolution on this material level has yet to be completed. It depends on man's own will to progress and may take as many thousands of years to reach perfection. At the same time homo sapiens is slowly being made aware of other inner and higher levels of consciousness. Whilst material consciousness appears so important to mankind, the development of this inner awareness of Self is retarded. Until that step in evolution is accomplished mankind has perforce to obey the laws which govern it – thus to respect physical boundaries. The law of cause and effect is one of these. As man sows (thinks and acts) in this limited awareness, so will he set in force a chain of events which will seek fulfilment. At the present stage of evolution man cannot avoid this. Hence what you term the law of karma.

But the statement 'divine grace transcends the law of karma' does not refer to the material suggestion of a vague act of forgiveness and pardon. Divine grace refers to the higher consciousness to which humanity is so slowly and painfully awakening. When man has reached this higher awareness by his slow acceptance of the spirit within him, when after trial and tribulation and the reaping of what he has sown, he has learned to live in the spirit whilst in the material body, then his state of evolution in matter will have reached its pinnacle and 'divine grace' (his progressed consciousness) will transcend the law of karma. Only few individuals have so far achieved this 'divine state', and they are not required to reincarnate.

There is a text in the Bible which says 'Him that overcometh will I make a pillar in the temple of the Lord, and he shall go no more out'.[1] This means that when we come to that pinnacle of living in divine grace whilst still in the body, then we will go not out any more. This is what 'divine grace transcending . . .' means.

There are two laws of evolution which are going on at the same time. The law of cause and effect. And the realisation of, and living in, the higher law of the spirit, divine grace.

In one of the Gospels Jesus is recorded as saying 'All things whatsoever ye pray and ask for, believe that ye have received them, and ye shall have them'.

What does this imply when one is praying for someone (who is in trouble) or for peace (say, in the Middle East)? It seems non-sense to pray as if the trouble had been resolved or peace had been established. And yet . . .?

There are two aspects of this question. The first one is the question of time. Time was invented by man; time is the blanket which closes much of his thoughts away from the Divine. Time is the creator of much that is troublesome, worrying and non-divine on this earth. When people leave this planet they pass out of time; there is no time in the spiritual world, all is one.

The second aspect is the matter of consciousness. Jesus spoke those very words, but from his divine consciousness, from the cosmic consciousness with which he was in tune – from the cosmic consciousness where there is no time, where everything is now, where the divine law works out. Man, unable to understand him, translated what he said into the concrete consciousness of this planet. That has been the great flaw in understanding the message and mission of Jesus.

Cosmic consciousness is the consciousness of the spirit now, and it is extremely difficult for those living on this earth plane to work in that consciousness. There have been great men who have experienced this consciousness, and their whole lives have been transformed. But usually consciousness is concrete, is held in time. Jesus also said, 'When you pray, go into your chamber and close the door' – at least that is how what he said has been translated. But Jesus, speaking from his cosmic understanding meant 'Go into yourself, close away the concrete consciousness of this lower plane, and try to ascend into a higher state of consciousness.' And it was from his cosmic consciousness that Jesus said 'When you pray for a thing (and I am putting it into simple words), believe that you have received that thing and give thanks for it.' That has always been a stumbling block in the Christian religion. Most people pray only for themselves or for something they want. Often it is not a high request, it is a selfish wanting on the plane of the material. Jesus did not mean that. And this is where mistakes have been made.

You have asked whether you should pray for peace in the Middle East, and then give thanks that it has happened. But that is the consciousness of the concrete world. For as you pray for that peace you know perfectly well within yourself that those men are not going to stop hating each other or envying each other or fighting each other. You are therefore praying against yourself, you are praying on the concrete level, on the lower level of the mind. But on the cosmic level, the divine law is being worked out, the divine plan is already accomplished [*on its own plane*. What remains to be accomplished are matters of timing and modalities on the physical plane. cf. The allegory of the architect on pp. 99–100]. Therefore if you prayed that men's minds would be lifted into the understanding of the divine law, you would be praying towards the cosmic level. At that level you could be thanking God, because it is already done. But that level will take time (your time) to work out. For centuries you have in your earth plane hated, envied, fought. You have fought wrongly, you have planned wrongly, you have lived wrongly. You are now reaping that karma which is yours but which is not in the cosmic consciousness at all. If you send out a thought or a prayer that there may be peace you are not touching the very source you wish to touch. Would it not be following the Master's injunction if you prayed 'May thy will be done. May the divine law work out'? Because that divine law is peace.

If you pray through the power of the Christ within every man, that his understanding, his consciousness be lifted, you are praying as the Master taught. You are then lifting men's minds into harmony, into understanding of each other's needs, into love that will bring peace. If you are praying for a helper in the work that you are trying to do, or for the place that you need for that work, and if you give thanks for it on the concrete level, your prayer is on that level and you are remaining on that level. The right way to pray would be, as Jesus taught, to go into your centre and lift your thoughts, and pray that all will be given for the work that you have to do. That help will come in the right way, because the divine law has already worked out your plan, the plan for you and for your work. It is in the hands of the divine consciousness, and give thanks that it has already happened.

In your prayer you were trying to materialise a concrete person or place. But this is not for you to do. By praying that the divine law will operate to provide all that is needed for your work, you are opening yourself to the divine law. And by thanking God for that power and that love and that assistance, you are, by the law of attraction, attracting to yourself the right person and the right place. It is a question of consciousness and time. Yet there is no time. So if you say 'We have been praying for weeks and it has not happened', you are closing it in with the blanket of time. God power, cosmic consciousness, has its own law, and that law works out in a divine way, the way which Jesus tried to show people on this planet. This way is to lift yourselves into that understanding of the divine law by saying to yourselves 'This is my work; this is what I have come to do. I ask only that all help from the spirit will be given, that all that is necessary and useful and helpful will be brought at the right time.' Then leave it, knowing that the law of attraction will attract the right person and the right place without your making it a concrete fact. Men and women on this planet are so enmeshed in the concrete, in the material life, that they do not realise that that is simply a working out of the plan and a working out of their own wrong thinking. Today your world is full of fear. And because man has brought that fear upon himself, it must go on to its fulfilment. But by praying that God's divine law for this planet is fulfilled and brought into manifestation, you are helping to bring about peace. By praying that the minds of men are lifted, that their consciousness is enlarged and widened, you are praying that peace will come in its right appointed way.

It is a difficult subject; indeed, it has been a most difficult subject for the last two thousand years.

[An implication of what is said about time in this very difficult communication is considered in Chapter 7.]

What is the place of recreation?
Recreation is laughter and happiness, and happiness and laughter are of the spirit. One should be thankful to God for the ability to enjoy the things of this earth. Jesus said, 'Render unto Caesar the things that are Caesar's, and unto God the things that are God's.' Render unto this world the things of this world and enjoy them in the right way. Enjoy your lives, your contacts, so long as they are harmless to others, and render under God those precious moments of understanding and oneness.

Some Comments on the Quoted Extracts
At the beginning of this chapter it was suggested that there are important criteria which teaching from an unknown source must satisfy if it is to be taken seriously.

Whether or not these criteria are satisfied is up to the reader to decide.

Of these extracts/communications, few, if any, are inconsistent with the model outlined in Chapter 4, and many provide powerful supporting evidence.

Teachers – about Themselves

The Teachers tell us that they have all passed through a school of human life, and so have first hand experience and understanding of the problems confronting humanity, both as individuals and collectively. Though the Teachers are masters of the purely human phase of evolution, they have not yet mastered what lies beyond and still have far, very far, to go. There is, in fact, no foreseeable end. For manifested life is *ever-becoming*.

A seeming inconsistency in the statements – 'We stand at the top', and 'there are planes beyond ours' – can be very easily resolved by reflecting that the 'Mount of Illumination' up which we are now climbing is probably no more than a quite minor peak in the great *cosmic* range.

The Present World Crisis – Foreseeing the Future – The New Age

In relation to this tremendous theme, one or two points stand out and evoke comment.

Between now and the end of this century there are likely to be far-reaching disturbances (cf. Matthew's Gospel, Chap. 24) due to a reaping by humanity of what humanity itself has sown. But the future is not foreordained – not totally anyway – and will be determined by how humanity thinks, feels, and acts, *now and in the future*. There are current today many prophecies. These are mainly of doom and disaster, either natural (e.g. cataclysms) or man made (e.g. wars), though a few are euphoric about the imminence of a new age when humanity's consciousness will be transformed and all that is bad will be swept away. The extracts indicate a middle course between these two extremes, although even the Teachers, with their greatly extended vision, cannot be certain whether what they foresee will actually come to pass. The extracts do, however, make it abundantly clear that a shift in consciousness, a change from the present worship of money and power, to a love of the eternal values (beauty, truth, and goodness), respect for nature and all that lives, and a heartfelt realisation that we are all children of one God, is essential if major disasters are to be averted.

Regarding prophecies and the role of prophecy, J. R. Jochmans in *Rolling Thunder* makes the following important observations:

A wise soothsayer once said that a prophecy that is completely fulfilled is a prophecy that has *failed*. It is a failure because the true revelation of the future is to both *warn and to instruct*.

The pattern of things to come as foretold by the prophets and seers of the world reveals that we shall eventually enter into what many call a 'New Age' – a time when the dreams of peace and brotherhood and spiritual understanding will finally be realised. This is the inevitable outcome toward which mankind is heading; the ultimate goal toward which history is moving. But between now and then must come a Transition, a metamorphosis from how we exist now, to how we shall be. For this Transition period, the prophets have predicted dramatic, often tragic and cataclysmic events. That the Transition is necessary, there is no doubt, but the degree to which changes will take place is what can be altered, if we so choose. The dire prophecies concerning famine, war, earth upheavals, religious persecution, chaos and other world disasters do *not* have to take place with the severity foreseen – in fact, *they do not have to take place at all*.

In reality, all prophecies of doom and gloom are conditional; that is they will take place only if the participants to whom the prophecy is given remain on the course they are on now. But if there is a change of heart, if the participants take positive action to move into another higher avenue of consciousness, then the prophecy need not come about – and thus its purpose, to generate change in men's minds, will be accomplished.[2]

98

By way of illustration Jochmans cites the Biblical story of Jonah and the whale. Jonah was instructed by God to prophesy to the citizens of Nineveh the imminent destruction of their city. Jonah's initial reaction was a refusal to do this, and to evade his responsibilities by leaving the city. In the Biblical story Jonah went to sea, fell overboard in a storm, was swallowed by a whale, and three days later was spewed out on the beach near Nineveh. After this experience Jonah decided to comply with God's request. And this he did indeed during the forty days preceding the prophecied catastrophe. Then, nothing happened! The reason? Jonah's warnings had been so successful that the inhabitants of Nineveh, or some of them anyway, had sufficiently changed their outlook and way of life that there was no need for the prophesied destruction. As Jochmans says in his book: 'The prophecy had failed in its fulfilment, but had won in *getting men to change themselves, rather than let events around them force them to change.'*

An arresting phrase in the extracts is: 'We see the plan going forth, and we shall continue to see the plan going forth.' After making due allowance for a change of wording, this phrase occurs several times. What does it mean? In particular, what is 'the plan'? Put very simply on p. 82, it is that 'people should be shown spiritual vision – that the ultimate purpose of life, the ultimate meaning of community, the ultimate understanding of a group, should be seen as the raising of man from the personal, through the psychical, to the spiritual'. Accepting this as the plan, how do we interpret the phrase 'We see the plan going forth.' To throw light on the problem raised by this question, an allegory may be helpful.

Consider an architect, let us suppose of a great cathedral, his mind focussed on some archetypal pattern or idea which he wants the building to symbolise. Though such an archetypal pattern or idea does not exist in space or time as normally understood, it will remain in being throughout the process of designing and constructing the actual building. It will permeate the minds of the designers, and may even percolate the consciousness of the builders. In so far as the drawings of the designers and, via them, the work of the builders conform to the will of the architect, all proceeds in harmony. But if the work of the designers and builders does not conform to the will of the architect, there will be disharmony, and what has been done may have to be undone, preparatory to tackling the task afresh.

In this allegory the architect represents the Lord of the World, the God of this planet, and the architect's archetypal pattern or idea corresponds to the Lord of the World's plan for the evolution of life on this planet. His will is the Law. When there is conformity with the Law, all proceeds in harmony. But when the Law is broken, disharmony occurs which may result in destruction and disaster. Like the designers and builders of the cathedral, humanity possesses freewill and so can choose whether or not to obey the Law.

Just as the cathedral architect's archetypal pattern and idea persists throughout the design and construction of the actual building, so does the plan of the Lord of the World remain in being throughout the evolution of life on this planet. This point is made very clearly on p. 87. 'It is the will of God, the will of the great Creator, to give all free will. Therefore his design, his purpose, may be blocked by the selfishness of the people to whom he has given free will. On the other hand, the purpose that is in the mind of the Creator will go forward, whatever happens. You are bound by time. We look ahead to where there is no time. What you may expect in the course of another hundred years may not occur within another thousand. But the purpose and design of evolution will not be changed.'

On an apparent inconsistency in the statements – 'Man is allowed to go his own way – up to a point. Now that point is nearly reached', and 'They are left as dead planets, planets without life yet where life has been. Let not this happen to this most beautiful planet of earth' – light can be thrown by considering school as an allegory. Suppose that a group of anti-social pupils is acting in a way which may set the school on fire. There are then three possibilities. The staff may intervene too late or unsuccessfully. The staff may intervene successfully. The school authorities may decide to close the school in part or in toto (cf. the flood which ended the great Atlantean civilization?) to be reopened maybe when the situation has changed. The real world correspondence would be a natural catastrophe of cataclysmic proportions – an 'act of God' to save the planet. Regarded as an allegory the above can be applied quite simply to each of the extracts.

The Soul – its Existence and Nature
In the mystery schools of the ancient world great importance was attached to the injunction 'Man know thyself', i.e. 'Man know thy Self'. In the East, too, in Hinduism and Buddhism, enquiry into the nature of the 'I', the self, has played a vital part in the thinking of these two religions. In the West, by contrast, emphasis has been on action, and it is only recently, maybe as a result of growing familiarity with Eastern thought, that the problem of identity, the mystery of the self, has become the subject of serious study and reflection.

The reasons for thinking that man is triune – personality, soul, and spirit – were discussed at length in *The Sacred Quest* and so will not be repeated here. Suffice it to say that the evidence for such a conclusion – cumulative evidence drawn from many different sources and traditions – is weighty. But establishing, at least with a high degree of probability, the existence of a deep centre, higher self or soul, is one thing; to describe its nature is another, and raises problems of a quite different order because of the impossibility of explaining the higher in terms of the lower. Since by definition, the soul transcends the personality, its consciousness is at a level of being which transcends physical sensing, emotional feeling, and discursive thinking. How then can we proceed? A partial, albeit very partial, answer is to consider statements by 'teachers' who are conscious at the soul level, and to take note of ostensible communications from those who, after physical death, have 'died' to their personality, i.e. have undergone the second death and are at one with their souls. Such statements or communications which have some claim to credibility are rare: hence the importance of what is said on pp. 74, 75 and 81 *et seq.*

About the overall validity of these communications the writer is not qualified to comment. For the reader they will either ring true – however disturbing their content and implications – or not. And of this the reader alone can be the judge.

A key sentence in a non-quoted communication is 'The sacrifice of personality is the "burnt offering" so little understood and means the relinquishing of selfishly oriented motives for the good of the whole – starting with the group.' In other words the replacement of I wish or I want, or I don't wish or I don't want – for myself, by a heartfelt concern for what the group stands for: a group, in this context consisting of people linked by a common concern and unity of purpose *in relation to an activity which benefits the whole*, in contrast to a group whose members are united by the common aim of fostering the purely personal desires and interests of individual members. While it is clear that in practice most groups do not fit neatly into either category but are a mixture of the two, it is equally clear that if groups were to subordinate the interests of their individual members to the good of all, to the wellbeing of the whole (of which the group may be only a very small part), the gravity of today's problems, both national and international, would be greatly and immediately reduced. This fact – a fact which few would dispute – shows the change which attitudes must undergo if the world's future is to be one of peace, brotherhood, and spiritual understanding. As Bertrand Russell puts it in *Roads to Freedom* –

> It is not the State, but the community, the worldwide community of all human beings, present and future, that we ought to serve . . . And a good community does not spring from

the glory of the State, but from the unfettered development of individuals . . . It is the individual in whom all that is good must be realised, and the free growth of the individual must be the supreme end of a political system which is to refashion the world.

At the individual level there are three stages. The first stage is essentially self-centred. What the 'I' wants and desires dominates. Moreover, wants and desires include happiness as well as possessions. The next stage is a gradual realisation of the need for unselfishness, for displacing the ego, the 'I', from its position of dominance. The resulting conflict is tellingly described in the following passage from *Discipleship in the New Age* –

> I presume you will recognise the truth of what I say when I express the opinion that your individual or personal love of humanity and the focus of your attention upon human need is very largely theoretical. It is transitory and experimental in practice. Your intentions are good and fine but you have not yet the *habit* of correct orientation and much that you do is the result of imposed sacrifice and at a cost; it is not natural to you; it is still the result of hopeful endeavour; you are still bewildered over the problem of how to be oriented to the Hierarchy and your soul, and at the same time to be oriented to humanity and your fellow men. *But the time will come when you are personally so decentralised that automatically the sense of 'others' is far stronger in you than the sense of personality or of the lower self.*[3]

The third stage is when the italic passage in the above extract (italicised by the writer) has become fact. This betokens a very significant shift in consciousness, marks the birth of the Christ within the heart, and indicates a soul-infused personality. Reaching this stage is the mark of being 'born again', the true 'second birth'.

Reincarnation and Karma
There is little to be said about these two inter-linked concepts by way of comment except to emphasise their importance.

Initiation
Anything said about this subject must perforce be second hand, and so should be treated with reserve. If what was said in relation to the allegory of the school in Chapter 4 is correct, namely, that the vast majority of the human race are in the second and third forms and that the number in the fifth and sixth forms, the forms in which examinations are taken, is very very small, then for all but the few, initiation lies in the far distant future.

According to tradition, the first five initiations are called Birth, Baptism, Transfiguration, Crucifixion or Great Renunciation, and Revelation. And whatever ceremony may be involved takes place in 'a temple not made with hands'. Initiation is not a reward for 'being good', but a recognition of what has been referred to as a shift in consciousness. Initiation consolidates and extends this expansion of consciousness and leads to work of greater responsibility and importance – as viewed by the Hierarchy if not by the general public who may be totally unaware of the work in question.

Jesus; Christ; the Lord of the World
The references in the extracts, though not very numerous, are highly significant, e.g.

> All the weeds that have grown up round that sacred tree, planted by the Initiate Jesus, have to be cut down and burned, so that the Tree of Life, the power which is within each soul, begins to flower.

> The divine laws which were given through the Hebrew prophets, and which were fulfilled and taught and lifted into grace by the Master of all the Masters, the Christ.

> Learn that naught matters in the infinitude of time and space excepting that which will aid the Lord of the World in His purpose.

The writer is well aware that this is a highly contentious and extremely sensitive area. Suffice it to say that the above statements seem to be consistent with the suggestions put forward in Chapter 4. See also Chapter 7.

Time

What is said about time in the answer given on pp. 93 *et seq.* is very difficult. But anyone who may be tempted to dismiss what is said as nonsense should bear in mind the following:

> In any attempt to bridge the domains of experience belonging to the spiritual and physical sides of our nature, Time occupies the key position.[4]
>
>   . . . Eddington

> Now he has departed from this strange world a little ahead of me. That is nothing. People like us, who believe in physics, know that the distinction between past, present and future is only a stubbornly persistent illusion.[5]
>
>   . . . Einstein (in a letter of condolence)

> It is this thought of the existence of Time itself, of its reality, of the fact that there is no time, that can begin to change the feeling of oneself in relationship to one's life.[6]
>
>   . . . Maurice Nicoll

> The Australian aborigines (and many other primitive societies) also conceive of two kinds of time. The first is our irresistible, passing time. The second is 'the Great Time' . . . It is the time of all-at-once instead of the time of one-thing-after-another. What occurs in the Great Time has sequence, but it cannot be dated as to *when* it happened. The time concept of the sensitive and of the mystic seems structurally akin to the primitives' concept of the Great Time.[7]
>
>   . . . Lawrence LeShan

References

1. Revelation 3:12
2. *Rolling Thunder*, J. R. Jochmans, (Sun Publishing Company, Albuquerque, U.S.A. 1980)
3. *Discipleship in the New Age*, Alice A. Bailey, (Lucis Publishing Company, 1944)

4. Quoted in *The Imprisoned Splendour*, Raynor C. Johnson, (Hodder & Stoughton, 1953), p. 148
5. Quoted in *Disturbing the Universe*, Freeman Dyson, (Harper & Row, 1979)
6. *Living Time and the Integration of the Life*, Maurice Nicoll, (Watkins, 1981), p. 89
7. *The Medium, the Mystic, and the Physicist*, Lawrence LeShan, (Turnstone Press, 1974), p. 50

Part II

The Significance of Part I

The need for a new metaphysic – to which reference was made in the Prologue on p. v – was discussed at length in *The Sacred Quest*. There it was argued that the need has arisen from the lack of any generally agreed long term goal for the future of human life on this planet. Without such a goal which recognises the spiritual, as well as material, aspects of man's being, the concept of a continuously rising material standard of living has assumed pride of place, in practice if not in theory, as the be-all and end-all of existence. Though raising the material standard of living is undoubtedly very important, especially for countries in which a significant proportion of the population lack adequate food, clothing, shelter, and medical attention, it will not satisfy as an overall long term goal once these basic needs are met. What should be means to an end has become an end in itself. When this happens – mistaking means for ends – trouble is never far behind.

The significance of Part I is that it provides a new metaphysic of very general application, some implications of which for religion, science, and man in society, are considered in the next three chapters.

7: Some Implications for Religion

The subject is so vast that we shall limit our observations to a consideration of matters raised by the three fundamental questions – 'Who or what is God?', 'Who or what is man?', 'What is the purpose of human life?', – and to an appraisal of the changes in present attitudes which are called for by the 'model' or new metaphysic suggested in Chapter 4. Pivotal in this appraisal is the concept of serial existence, reincarnation in its little understood form. If the concept is valid, at least in essentials, fundamental rethinking over a whole range of important topics is inescapable. If it is not, the model put forward in Chapter 4 collapses. In the remainder of this chapter, for reasons that have been discussed at length in previous chapters, it will be assumed that reincarnation embodies a profound truth.

'Who or what is God?' That God cannot be defined is obvious and not in question. But the time has surely come when, on an increasing number of occasions, we need to be more explicit about who or what we are referring to when we use the word God. As pointed out in Chapter 4, the word is used in at least four different ways in conventional Christian thinking. To denote the Absolute, THAT from which *all that is* proceeds. To connote that great Being in whom in very truth we live and move and have our being, the Lord of the World, the God of this planet. To describe Christ – the Second Person of the Christian Trinity. To describe Jesus. In much conventional current thinking, Jesus and Christ are one and the same; hence the frequent reference to Jesus Christ or Christ Jesus. Two most serious sources of confusion centre round (a) the failure to distinguish between the Absolute and the Lord of the World, and (b) the failure to differentiate between Jesus and Christ. In relation to (a) W. R. Inge, a former Dean of St. Paul's, said 'The God of religion is not the ineffable Absolute, but the God Who reveals Himself to man in the creation and in the human soul. In prayer we speak to Him as to a Being Who can hear and answer us. Such intercourse could not be held with the Godhead, the Absolute.'[1]

About THE ABSOLUTE there is much confusion. The only assertion that can be made concerning life and all that is included in that term which never changes is that it IS. IS-NESS is THE ABSOLUTE, the only principle in the whole of life that cannot be modified, abolished, or exchanged for something else. Closest to THE ABSOLUTE is the abstract principle of *Being*, or what may be termed LIFE. LIFE is *being*, infinite and eternal, but not *a* being, nor yet the collective hierarchies of beings that constitute the manifested universe. For all these are but limited expressions of it. LIFE is the unmanifest *Logos* of the Greek philosophers. It is that which is called 'The Word' at the beginning of St John's Gospel. 'The Word was with God' means that it is that which is nearest to THE ABSOLUTE, the unknowable Principle of IS-NESS and, like it, is in its actuality, eternally unknowable. Yet LIFE, though eternal and infinite, is not absolute, for it reveals itself in an infinitude of modifications of itself, whereas IS-NESS is subject to no modifications whatsoever. LIFE possesses a single attribute, the quality of EVER-BECOMING. P. G. Bowen expresses it thus:

[THAT] . . . into which all appearances eternally pass and are lost is LIFE. The eternal procession of its aspects eternally vanishing into the Noumenon, LIFE itself, is the EVERBE-COMING, the 'eternal, ceaseless motion' of the real Universe. LIFE is; but it is manifest only in its sole attribute, EVERBECOMING.[2]

In the above, words and terms printed in capitals refer to the ultimate and noumenal nature of beings, things and conditions.

Great Beings, of whom the Lord of the World is one, and of whom planets, suns, solar systems, perhaps even constellations, may be regarded as bodies of manifestation, are probably many. And an appreciation of this is important. Because it replaces an earth-centred concept of the universe by something rather different. It also replaces the very prevalent and, on reflection, presumptuous assumption that humanity is the most evolved form of life within the solar system by the realisation that humanity is probably nothing of the kind. Much more likely is the proposition that within the solar system human consciousness occupies some middle position in the spectrum of life. Indeed, if the esoteric tradition is correct in asserting that within the cosmos there are seven great bands of consciousness and that at present human consciousness is functioning in the seventh, lowest, of these bands, everything points to humanity having far, very far, to go! It is not, of course, being suggested that there is life on other planets analogous to life on earth and visible to physical sight. The idea being put forward is the possibility that within the solar system there are evolving hierarchies of self-conscious beings who exist in realms, separate from but analogous to, the 'inner worlds' associated with the earth. One of the Teachers referred to in Chapter 6 said on one occasion 'The earth is only part of a far far larger scheme [than just the Earth].' There is an esoteric tradition that of the evolving hierarchies of beings within the solar system, earth humanity is the one most deeply embedded in matter and involved in suffering, and that the earth is referred to as 'the sorrowful planet' on that account.

And what about intermediaries between man and the Lord of the world? Those, maybe, who are referred to in the Prayer Book as 'angels and archangels and all the company of heaven'. Is it not time that the existence of such beings was recognised and their role understood? I know of two people, one a trained clairvoyant, the late Mrs P. D. Bendit, the other a close friend of unusual sensitivity, who have 'seen' a great angelic being. One was at the critical moment in an important ceremony, the other was during a big thunderstorm.

One of the limitations experienced by humanity at its present stage of evolution is in relation to space and time, especially the latter. On pages 99 and 100, in order to throw light on the phrase 'We see the plan going forth', reference was made to the concept, design, and construction of a cathedral, treated as an allegory. As a commentary on space and time, we shall now consider this allegory in rather more detail. Focussing on bare essentials, the people concerned comprise the architect – one person; designers – relatively few; and craftsmen – a large number. The architect has, we shall assume, some great concept which he wishes the building to symbolise. Such a concept, corresponding perhaps to what Plato would have called an 'idea' and Jung an 'archetype', does not really exist in space or time as normally understood. The concept or 'idea' exists in a timeless state within the architect's mind.

The task of the designers is to translate the architect's concept or 'idea' into detailed plans and working drawings. Preparatory to producing these in their final form, a designer will 'turn things over in his mind', and, when doing so, will be working in 'subjective space' and 'subjective time'. (cf. a speaker preparing a lecture. He 'turns over in his mind' what he is going to say and when doing so is often totally oblivious of the ticking of the clock.) Not until the plans and working drawings are completed do space and time become objective.

The role of the craftsmen is to build according to the detailed plans and blueprints of the designers. So long as these are adhered to all is well. But if the craftsmen go off on their own and build according to their own likes and dislikes irrespective of the detailed plans and blueprints of the designers, what they build will come to nought and will eventually have to be taken down and rebuilt.

In this allegory the architect is the Lord of the World, 'the one who sees the end from the beginning'; the designers are the Teachers; and the craftsmen are the ordinary men and women of today. The purpose of the allegory is twofold. First, to indicate the existence of different kinds of time. Second, to indicate humanity's place in the scheme of things.

In the Jewish tradition preceding the Christian era, it was not uncommon for God to be thought of in the image of man, manifesting the whole range of man's personal qualities, both good, such as mercy and justice, and not so good, like anger and jealousy. With the coming of Jesus, the picture changed. Jesus taught the masses to regard God as a loving Father, but without any of the weaknesses associated with an ordinary human father. And today? For many the image of God is still of a person. But what is so often lacking is an appreciation of the well known passage from Isaiah. 'For my thoughts are not your thoughts, neither are your ways my ways, saith the Lord. For as the heavens are higher than the earth, so are my ways higher than your ways, and my thoughts than your thoughts.'[3] At humanity's present stage of development, consciousness is predominantly emotional and self-centred. 'I wish or I want, and I don't wish or I don't want – for myself.' And this attitude is projected on to God. With the result that because we are so concerned with our personal desires and with the happiness which we think will follow their realisation, we consider that God's attitude will be in accord. But is this really so? Consider the following verse from The Epistle to the Hebrews – 'My son, regard not lightly the chastening of the Lord, nor faint when thou art reproved of him: for whom the Lord loveth he chasteneth.'[4] Though God cannot want us to be unhappy, His prime concern, surely, is not that we should be happy, but that we should develop spiritually. And this implies a shift in consciousness; a replacement of our desire to be happy through realising our predominantly self-centred wants and desires by a determination to align our personal will with the divine will, success in doing which leads to joy. An important consequence of this is in relation to petitional prayer; by appreciating the need to ensure, in so far as we are able, that what we pray for is not just for the satisfaction of our personal desires and wants but is in accordance with the divine will. At a recent conference in Japan, the leader of the American Indian Sioux people said 'Be careful what you pray. God takes your prayers very seriously.' In the words of Meister Eckhart: 'Perfectly to will what God wills, to want what he wants, is to have joy; but if one's will is not quite in unison with God's, there is no joy.'[5]

Another area which calls for fundamental reappraisal is that of sin and guilt, repentance and forgiveness. The existence of sin – 'missing the mark', and of evil – the deliberate flouting of God's will, is all too obvious, both individually and nationally. And so too is their importance.[6] But what about guilt and forgiveness? It does not require much study of the Old Testament to appreciate the extent to which the Jews were weighed down by feelings of sin and guilt, and by their anxiety to obtain forgiveness from an angry and menacing Jehovah. To meet this deeply felt need, the blood sacrifices deemed necessary to atone for sin and thereby obtain Jehovah's forgiveness were formalised and codified. And the law which resulted came to play a very important part in the life of the Jewish people. At certain periods in their history keeping the letter of the law assumed greater importance than expressing such qualities as mercy and justice, the absence of which had called the law into being in the first place. But when this happened there arose prophets who saw all too clearly what was happening and said so in no uncertain terms. Then came Jesus, who said 'Think not that I came to destroy the law or the prophets: I came not to destroy but to fulfil',[7] though his subsequent remark 'Think not that I came to send peace on the earth: I came not to send peace, but a sword'[8] implied that fulfilment would involve the destruction of much that was false. It is not altogether surprising therefore that the Christian tradition has incorporated some of the Old Testament attitudes of sin and guilt, repentance and forgiveness. For example, some of the wording of the General Confession and the

114

Prayer of Consecration. The magnitude of Christ's sacrifice in entering into human form and the inestimable value of his life in showing us the 'Way' are not in question. But it seems to be assumed by many that as a result of Jesus Christ's life and more especially death the *consequences* of our sins – the occasions when we have 'missed the mark' – have been rendered null and void. This is a very different matter and surely cannot be.

To clarify the situation let us consider an analogy. A and B are two people, of whom A has done B a grave wrong. And let us suppose that A is sincerely sorry, is determined not to repeat the offence, has expressed his deep regret to B, and has asked for B's forgiveness. If B is an ordinary person – not particularly good or noble – it is almost certain that he will accept A's apology. But that does not imply that A will not feel under a very strong obligation to make good, to the best of his ability, whatever it was that he did wrong. And if that applies to A and B, two ordinary human beings, how infinitely more will it apply if B is replaced by God.

Deeply embedded within the Christian tradition is the feeling of guilt, and that we shall only be forgiven if we debase ourselves and adopt a 'miserable sinner' attitude. If, as is being suggested, human life on this planet can be likened to life at school, 'a miserable sinner' attitude to our shortcomings is neither appropriate nor healthy. To be humble and acknowledge our shortcomings is one thing, and eminently good; but to grovel is another, and far from good. That we 'miss the mark', i.e. make mistakes, is certainly regrettable, but virtually inevitable. What matters, having made a mistake, is to admit the mistake, understand what we did wrong and why, endeavour to make amends for whatever it was that we did wrong, and then be prepared and ready to become involved in a comparable situation and, this time, to act rightly (in thought, word, and deed). For only thus can we demonstrate that we have understood and mastered our earlier weakness. But to compress such a process into one life is manifestly not possible. Hence the relevance and importance of serial existence, together with the allied concept of karma, the law of ethical causation. Although karma is usually regarded as an Eastern concept, the statement of Jesus recorded in each of the first three Gospels 'In whatsoever measure ye mete, it shall be measured to you again' constitutes a remarkably succinct description of the karmic principle. It is *not* a matter of punishment, as is so often thought, but the provision of an environment *in which we can learn our much needed lessons.* As the teacher says to his pupil in *The Wheel of Rebirth*:

> A great many things seem unfair to people with such limited vision as yours. But you need not disturb yourself; nothing that is permitted by those Great Ones, the Lords of Karma, can be anything but just, since it is apportioned in exact accordance with the law of Cause and Effect. Nothing that man has ever done or thought escapes Them; They are the weavers of the multitudinous threads of man's destiny; They hold the balances of perfect justice and truth; . . . Do not forget, no task is ever given, no trial is ever allowed to man, greater than he is able to undertake or to bear. His capacities are ever gauged to a hair's breadth. Often his Higher Self is consulted before the birth of its personality as to whether it is willing to risk the heavy karma of failure. If only man would grasp the fact that everything that happens to him, good or ill, is basically his own deliberate choice, and that he can always be greater than what he calls his fate! But how few live up to their potentialities – indolence and fear ever hold them back; yet there are in the universe infinite reserves of strength for him who struggles bravely on against apparently overwhelming odds.[9]

and

> Remember, any effort causes resistance, and resistance in man's body registers as pain. A large proportion of pains and sorrows come about by people resisting the Law of Karma and resenting the necessities that it imposes upon them; the cultivation of a balanced mind and a reasonable outlook would do much to mitigate this. When a man has succeeded in eliminating from his vehicles all discordant elements, so that every atom of all his bodies is vibrating in harmony with the

Divine Will, no activities on the physical or astral plane have any more the power to cause within him friction or disturbance. This is the secret of that perfect health, that inner peace and superabundant strength which the Great Ones have always possessed.[10]

Without in any way belittling the Christ, of whom more will be said presently, the present section, ending with the above quotations, does indicate that the interpretations which are currently given to the words 'forgiveness' and 'atonement', especially 'vicarious atonement', call for a very drastic rethink.

Another area in which it seems to the writer that there is great confusion is the need to distinguish between Jesus, Christ, and the Second Person (Aspect) of the Christian Trinity (Father, Son, and Holy Spirit). An ancient tradition affirms that two thousand years ago Jesus was a high initiate who was overshadowed by the Christ during the period of his Ministry, beginning with his baptism in Jordan by John the Baptist and ending with his crucifixion at Jerusalem three years later. The Christ is that Great Being who overshadowed Jesus during the years of his Ministry and has been referred to as 'World Teacher', 'the Master of all the Masters', and 'the first of earth humanity to achieve divinity in his own right'.[11] His human evolution was completed in the distant past, and two thousand years ago in Palestine he was as perfect a channel for the 'Son', the second aspect of the Lord of the World, as was possible within the extreme limitations of human incarnation. If, in broad essentials, this is correct – as was argued at some length in *The Sacred Quest* – it follows that the Gospel story is an intertwining, very hard to disentangle, of the sayings of Jesus, of the Christ speaking through Jesus, and perhaps even of inspiration proceeding directly from the Lord of the World, all set within the framework of a more or less historical account of the life of Jesus as actually lived. In *A Man Seen Afar*, W. Tudor Pole has this to say:

Jesus never seems to have made it clear to them (His Disciples) when he was speaking as an individual to individuals, and when the Christ was speaking through him – not so much to those present as to the countless generations yet unborn. In the middle of a conversation often about everyday affairs, his countenance would change, his delivery become compelling, authoritative. Then the words that issued forth would be addressed to all mankind in all ages . . . But those who were actually listening went on applying his prophecies and statements solely to themselves and to their own generation.

I am speaking of course, of the three years at the close of his short life when the Christ clothed and permeated his whole being. In earlier years he was very much a man among men, speaking a language they could understand, often eloquent, inspiring, but always simple. Not until he met John the Baptist did the immensity of the mission which lay ahead begin to dawn and then gradually to encompass him.

I feel certain that there are records still in existence, awaiting discovery, which will make clear the mystery of the Master's seemingly dual personality, and elucidate the change that took place within him in the waters of the Jordan, in his twenty-eighth year.[12]

Though this may seem complicated, it does provide a way forward from a position which is rapidly becoming untenable: to wit, that Jesus Christ, a single being, is both man and, at the same time, the 'only begotten Son of God' and on a par with the creator of the cosmos 'God the Father Almighty, Maker of heaven and earth, and of all things visible and invisible'. Moreover, without a lot of explanation, the situation is made still more difficult by the use of phrases such as 'Christ in you the hope of glory', and 'the Birth of the Christ within the heart'.

For Christians, one of the most hallowed and oft quoted sayings of Jesus is His reply to Thomas recorded in John's Gospel – 'I am the way, and the truth, and the life: no one cometh unto the Father, but by me.'[13] Within the framework of serial existence not only is this statement important, but it assumes much greater importance than is generally realised. For it means that not only must we have the faith that was expressed by Peter – 'Thou art the Christ, the Son of the Living God',[14] but it implies that attaining to the mind of Christ is in very truth the way we all have to go. For virtually everyone the way ahead will be long and arduous, and will involve many many lives of trial and error and the learning of lessons. For there are no short cuts and each has to tread the way himself. But eventually the end of the road will be reached, and 'Man will enter into his divine heritage and know himself as the Son of the Father, with all the divine characteristics, powers and capacities which are his because of his divine endowment.'[15]

It is now time to consider the question 'Who, or what, is man?' In Hinduism and Buddhism, what is the I (the first personal pronoun), has always been regarded as an appropriate point from which to start on the religious quest. In the Christian West the question has been but rarely asked until the recent influx of Eastern ideas. The West has been dominated by action as inspired by the life of Jesus; the East has been dominated by the reflections of its spiritual teachers. Noting the crippling poverty throughout so much of the East and the frenzied activity which permeates so much of the West, has not the time arrived when the two should be brought together? The allegory of the chariot described in Chapter 4 puts a somewhat different slant on the current attitude to the point and purpose of the spiritual life. For many Christians the primary motive for leading, or trying to lead, a spiritual life is to please God, though this is inevitably linked with a secondary motive, namely, to ensure, in so far as this is possible, a tolerably pleasant existence after death. The weakness of this condition is that if faith in God falters or belief in life after death grows dim, so does the incentive for leading a spiritual life. The allegory of the chariot in no way detracts from such motivation, but it sharpens it greatly by providing an at least partial explanation of the following cryptic but cogent pronouncements (quoted in Chapter 3).

119

(a)   Each man is his own absolute lawgiver, the dispenser of glory or gloom to himself; the decreer of his life, his reward, his punishment. (Hermetic)
(b)   All that we are is the result of what we have thought. (Buddhist)
(c)   Union (or Yoga) is achieved through the subjugation of the psychic nature, and the restraint of the mind. When this has been accomplished, the Yogi knows himself as he is in reality. (Hindu)
(d)   In whatsoever measure ye mete it shall be measured to you again. (Christian)

For an increasing number of people the concept of man as 'a being who is born *de novo*, maybe in pleasant surroundings and highly talented, maybe in uncongenial surroundings and severely handicapped, and who struggles through his (or, or course, her) allotted span until his disappearance from the human scene at death after which there is uncertainty and almost total ignorance', will not serve much longer. Just as science is prepared to discard the *forms* in which its apprehension of truth is expressed, so must religion.

The preceding sentence leads inevitably to the third fundamental question: 'What is the purpose of human life?' If, as was suggested in Chapter 4, human life on this planet resembles life at school – a term corresponding to an incarnation and the holidays to the period between – the purpose of human life becomes, in broad outline, relatively clear: to wit, that mankind should develop into truly mature men and women. And what does this imply? It means that it should be possible for such a one to perform in the great drama of life whatever part he (or, of course, she) is called upon to play with grace, skill, and selfless dedication. But this is not possible without an alteration in consciousness of a kind which for all but the few is still a long way off. A hint of what this involves is indicated by the following extracts from talks given by one of the teachers quoted in Chapter 6.

It is through sin, sorrow, selfishness, karma and pain that man evolves, and these leave their marks upon him as the shores of ancient seas are whitened and scarred for aeons of time after the waters have receded. It is the depth of understanding and the breadth of vision implicit in the evolutionary process towards which the disciple is led – through mires and miasmas, through pain and purification, and through deserts and disasters to the goal of fulfilment and to higher evolutionary stages where he can be more effective because he has acquired all states of consciousness. He is all things and fears no thing; he is a mystic but his feet are firmly on the ground; he is an occultist, a psychic and a disciple serving in the ashram of humanity's needs. He has mastered all states of awareness and so he learns to become a Master. The evolving disciple *knows* – but he does not insist on his ideas for he also knows that freedom of decision is the right of all men.

It is acceptance which is ever the key word. Disciples must accept *everything* – with joy and serenity. There is naught that may be excluded from this acceptance of aught that lies within the realm of conditions, circumstances and occurrences: *whatever it is*, it is the disciple's own karma and his own opportunity precipitated by his soul, or by his actions or his emotions reflecting back to him that which he expressed. Where he rejects, he has discarded another opportunity and challenge which could have taken him that little farther along the path, the path being the lighted way to greater subtlety and selflessness. Moreover, he has retarded the growth or progress of something that it was his opportunity to stimulate and expand – whether it was goodwill, consciousness, group interplay or simply his own karmic release. Acceptance may mean sacrifice – make it. Do you not know that sacrifice is the only way to true liberation? Do you suppose that Christ would have achieved His unequalled and unprecedented attainment without sacrifice? Would Jesus have taken His Initiation without the Cross? Or do you wait for some distant time and day when that momentous experience will be thrust upon you? Crucifixion is a daily affair and not something in the dim and distant future seen in the glamoured haze of awe. Crucifixion is the stabilising of the personality as the soul is allowed to influence the daily life in the three worlds of expression.

121

Sacrifice and acceptance are synonymous terms; ponder on this, allied to the thought that it is the means whereby the disciple achieves liberation and revelation of light from the prison of darkness.

References

1. Quoted in *Frontiers of Revelation*, Frances Banks, (Parrish, 1962), p. 139
2. *The Occult Way*, P. G. Bowen, (The Occult Book Society, 1938), p. 27
3. Isaiah 55:8
4. Hebrews 12:5
5. *Meister Eckhart*, translated by Raymond B. Blakney, (Harper & Row, New York, 1941). Talks of Instruction No. 23
6. Sin and evil, conscious and unconscious, are discussed in Chap. 15 of *The Sacred Quest*, (James Clarke, 1986)
7. Matthew 5:17
8. Matthew 10:34
9. *The Wheel of Rebirth*, H. K. Challoner, (Rider & Co. 1935, republished by the Theosophical Publishing House, 1969), p. 162
10. *Ibid.* p. 267
11. Discussed in the writings of Alice A. Bailey. See, in particular, *The Rays and the Initiations*, (Lucis Publishing Co., 1960). cf. Romans 8:29
12. *A Man Seen Afar*, W. Tudor Pole & Rosamond Lehmann, (Neville Spearman, 1965)
13. John 14:6
14. Matthew 16:16
15. *A Treatise on White Magic*, Alice A. Bailey, (Lucis Publishing Co., 1934), p. 327

8: Some Implications for Science

The implications for science of the model outlined in Chapter 4 might be summed up in Hamlet's oft-quoted observation: 'There are more things in Heaven and Earth, good Horatio, than are dreamt of in your philosophy.' In other words, quite a lot of observable events take place which are not consistent with scientific laws *as at present formulated*. Until very recently the great majority of scientists took the view that unless the events could be reproduced in a laboratory under controlled conditions, they were not interested. But paranormal events have not ceased happening, and some of them occur with such frequency, though not as yet in a laboratory, that to ignore them, on principle as it were, is verging on the ridiculous – the bending of knives and forks, for example, or events of which the following is more or less typical. It was the experience of a friend of many years standing who, at the time, was occupying a position of considerable responsibility. The account which follows is exactly as my friend recorded it. The event, of itself, was trivial, as is the bending of knives and forks, but it has implications which are anything but trivial. For assuming the event occurred as described, it shows that mind, incarnate and/or discarnate, can operate on matter directly. And thanks to the experimental work now being done by Professor Hasted, such an assumption is no longer without scientifically respectable supporting evidence.[1]

> It fell to my lot to live in a house which was visited almost daily by someone who was distinctly unbalanced, whose moods were unpredictable, and who had a very real 'chip on the shoulder'.

As I had never in my life experienced any type of poltergeist activity and only knew about it from hearsay, the following events took me completely by surprise. Though it is my firm conviction that any paranormal experience must be critically scrutinised with logical common sense before being treated as authentic and I applied this scrutiny on each occasion, I was always convinced that I was in fact witnessing a paranormal event.

On the first occasion I entered the house carrying a bundle of unfolded papers,one being the draft of an important letter I had been asked to type immediately. I sat down at the typewriter but this one sheet had gone from the bundle. I searched the room, all over the floor, and the outside hall and pathway, but it was nowhere to be found. I had a strange feeling that with sight a little above the physical I had noticed a piece of paper disappearing sideways from the bundle but had discounted it as illusion until I found it to be missing. I used the room daily, and a few days later I walked into it to find the letter neatly folded, lying on a chest where I never put any papers.

The second event occurred a few weeks later and involved my gold wristlet watch which at night time I always put on a shelf beside my bed, replacing it on my wrist after dressing in the morning. On this occasion I looked on the shelf but the watch was not there. I searched the entire room, naturally very concerned as the watch was valuable and had belonged to my sister. It happened to be the day when I put clean sheets on the bed which had been completely stripped. I therefore gave up the search as being hopeless. Towards the end of the day I found the watch carefully placed just under the bottom sheet at the place where one would open the bed to get into it.

On the third occasion I had been cleaning my carpet and just before finishing I placed the bottle of 1001 cleaner on the television set. The next time I looked, a few minutes later, it had gone. By now I was becoming used to these happenings and on each occasion I politely asked the entity to be kind enough to put the article back. Not more than half an hour later I was in the room with my back to the television set and thought I heard a very faint tinkling sound. I turned round and once more the bottle was standing on the television set.

The fourth occasion was witnessed by a friend and had a

humorous side to it. I had washed and hung out on the line a vest and pair of tights. Presently it started to rain. I was not there and a friend kindly brought in my washing and left it in the hall. I came in and found the vest but no tights. I thanked her for her kindness and asked her what she had done with the tights. These, she said, were wrapped up inside the vest. I shook the vest to show her that no tights were there. We searched the house and garden but the tights had disappeared. We went into the kitchen, which is not accessible from the garden and the tights were lying carefully spread out on the kitchen table. My friend was completely taken aback but I had by now become used to such events.

A characteristic of all these happenings was that the articles were always returned quite undamaged usually soon after their disappearance.

A friend who is knowledgeable in such matters was of the opinion that these little tricks were being played by a discarnate spirit, possibly that of a child, who wished to show me that they were concerned for my welfare and out to protect me from the evil vibrations of the unbalanced person who visited my house. An interesting sidelight to these strange happenings was a remark made to me by my small great-nephew, not quite four years old. He suddenly stopped in the middle of a game, looked at me very seriously and said 'There is darkness in your house'. I need hardly say he knew nothing of what had taken place, but obviously took a serious view of the situation he was picking up because he said again 'There is darkness in your house.'

With the departure for good of the disturbed person [to a different job in a different locality] all the paranormal activities ceased.

Looking at the world around us we notice that everything that is alive, be it vegetable, animal, or human, manifests through a form. So far as is known life without form does not occur, and form, unless it is animated by a coordinating life, is always in process of disintegration. Although this is only demonstrably true in relation to the world of the five physical senses, evidence provided by the trained clairvoyant, such as the late Mrs Bendit, indicates very strongly that the same applies to some, at least, of the 'inner worlds' as well. As explained in Chapter 4, this implies the existence of what was there referred to as emotional matter and mental matter or 'mind stuff', and that just as physical matter constituting our physical body is necessary for the functioning of our physical senses, so emotional matter constituting our emotional body is necessary for us to feel (emotionally), and mental matter constituting our mental body is necessary for us to think (discursively). In Chapter 4 it was pointed out that all three 'bodies' (or vehicles as they are referred to in the East) have a life of their own, and that all three 'bodies' are for us to train and use. The 'I' (the first personal pronoun), the self, the seat of the will, exists at an altogether deeper (subtler) level of being, a level at which many mystics tell us that space and time as we know them cease to be. But, even if true, what has this got to do with the influence of mind on matter? Let us see.

During this century physicists have shown that matter and energy are not the independent categories that they were once thought to be, so that when we talk about the physical body, we are talking about an intensely complex energy pattern. And this being so, is it not highly probable that the same applies to what we have called the emotional body and the mental body? And that they, too, can be regarded as intensely complex energy patterns. Now different energy patterns may, or may not, interact. Some do not, e.g. two water waves approaching each other head on pass through each other without interference; some do, e.g. two trains of sound waves which, when emitted from the same source but at different frequencies, reinforce each other at some points but cancel each other out at others.

In the case of a human being we are concerned with three energy fields – the physical, the emotional, and the mental – each having its own immensely complex pattern. The extent to which there may be interference between these fields we simply do not know, but there is no reason for thinking that it may not be very considerable. There may, for instance, be something analogous to resonance in the case of sound, so

126

that a condition of disharmony in one field may tend to produce a comparable condition in an adjoining field. Although this is certainly a gross oversimplification of what happens in practice, it may none the less throw some light on how mind can influence matter. Mind and matter are not the completely independent categories which they were once thought to be. Matter has a life aspect and life has a matter aspect. Hence the possibility of interaction.

During the last fifty years there have been a few, but only very few, attempts to find out whether there are energy fields surrounding the human body and, if so, what is their nature. Such work as has been done includes the experiments by the late Professor H. S. Burr of Yale Medical School which have been written up and published as *Blueprint for Immortality*,[2] and material contained in *Subtle Body*[3] and *Radionics and the Subtle Anatomy of Man*[4] by David Tansley, *The Loom of Creation*[5] – a study of the purpose and the forces that weave the pattern of existence – by Dennis Milner and Edward Smart, *The Awakened Mind*[6] by Maxwell Cade and Nona Coxhead, and *The Unseen Self* – an account of Kirlian photography – by Brian and Marita Snellgrove.[7] No attempt is made here to compare the relative merits of these approaches or to assess precisely what has been established, as the work is essentially in its initial stages. But these investigations are to be welcomed, most warmly, and having due regard to the possibilities of what may emerge it is a very great pity that in the U.K. so few professional skills and resources are being channelled into this particular field of enquiry. Although when undertaking a particular piece of research it is most unwise for the researcher to pin his (or, of course, her) hopes on what he *expects* to find, it is not unwise for him to keep an open mind regarding what he *may* find. And one such discovery could be the etheric – known variously as the etheric field, the etheric body, the health aura, the body of vitality, the linga sharira. Unlike, perhaps, what we have referred to as the emotional and mental bodies, it seems that the etheric exists within our familiar three dimensional space-time world, and that the etheric field can therefore be regarded as part, albeit a subtle and non-visible part, of the physical body. This is what the Western clairvoyant with extended physical sight (exceedingly rare) sees with his/her physical eyes and the Eastern mystic intuits, and maybe sees as well. It provides the field or structure upon which the physical body is built, and bears somewhat the same relationship to the physical body as the magnetic field of a magnet does to the iron filings on the laboratory bench. Although a more detailed account of the etheric field is contained in *The Sacred Quest*, a little of what was said there is repeated here because of the subject's importance.

General ill-health shows in the vital field as a whole, but local disease produces marked local changes as well as a disturbance of the whole. Thus a superficial cut or bruise is visible etherically as well as physically. There is a slight break in the rhythm of the vital currents over the site of the injury. Such things as malignant disease or abscess formation show both a generally deranged etheric field and a localised condition. This is often visible long before there is any evidence of organic trouble. It begins as a patch of disorganisation of the currents in the particular part of the field over the organ affected. The rhythmic flow becomes broken and irregular, and small vortices form in which, as in a river whirlpool, waste matter accumulates instead of being thrown out. The natural colour disappears, and the whole texture becomes denser as the waste material coagulates, just as mud is deposited by water. The movement slows down until real stagnation occurs. Then, at a certain point, the whole process becomes as it were precipitated into the level of the physical tissues and local organic disease is established.

Thought and feeling, not to mention profounder spiritual activity, are constantly reflected into the health aura, which changes from moment to moment as mental processes take place. There is an Indian saying that 'Prana [vitality] follows thought'. This is indeed seen to be a fact because there is an immediate alteration in the health aura as mood and thinking change.[8]

128

On the surface of the etheric field are seven force centres.

Each of these psychic organs, looked at clairvoyantly, ['clairvoyantly' is here being used to include extended physical sight] is described as roughly in the shape of a cornucopia, with its narrow end based at a critical point in the physical spinal cord, and its mouth extending to the edge of the etheric aura . . . The cornucopial shape is due not to a fixed structure but to the play of two streams of psychic energy weaving together. One of these, flowing in the spinal cord, is thrown out from the centre and flows towards the periphery in a widening spiral; this represents the motor stream. The second stream, impinging on the surface of the etheric body, spirals inward, narrowing as it goes; this is the receptive or sensory stream. These two spirals flow parallel to one another, but in opposite directions, and may be compared to interlocking screw-threads, in that one may be said to run in the grooves of the other. They give an impression of spinning, like the fluid in the vortex of a whirlpool. It is this characteristic rotary movement which gives these centres their Sanskrit name of 'chakras' or wheels.[9]

The chakras, or force centres, are of paramount functional importance, as they are in effect the organs by which psycho-spiritual man expresses himself in the etheric, and thence in the dense physical world. Taken collectively, they should be a balanced system, each one of which reflects a certain form of psychic activity; while taken together they are a manifestation of the whole of the individual in action. Nothing of non-physical man becomes effective in the dense worlds except through the chakras.[10]

From the above extracts it is not difficult to envisage the immense changes which the scientific recognition of the etheric field would bring to many aspects of medicine, both physical and psychological. Not only would it provide a prior warning about some lack of rhythm or harmony which will manifest as a disturbance in the physical body unless checked. It would also be able to show in what way certain patterns of thinking and, more particularly, feeling can affect the physical body. It would thus throw a flood of light on the psycho-somatic nature of a lot of illness.

An extension of the preceding topic which now comes up for consideration is the influence of thought and feeling, not just on the physical body but on the human environment. If mind can act on small material objects directly, i.e. without physical contact, can the mind affect in a comparable way, i.e. other than by physical contact, the physical environment? The logical answer must surely be that it can, at least in some measure. What does this imply? It adds substance to what many people have often felt: namely, that a negative (i.e. destructive) attitude of mind seems to precipitate negative conditions, while a positive (i.e. constructive) attitude of mind appears to promote positive conditions. Reverting to the analogy of the iron filings in a magnetic field, it is as if in the positive case the field was being reinforced and the iron filings therefore under increased pressure to 'line up', but as if in the negative case the reverse was happening. If this is in any way correct, it indicates just how important are our habitual states of thought and feeling, especially those which are clear, strong, and constant. (At our present stage of development, when the personal will is so often at odds with the divine will, it is probably just as well that most of our thoughts and feelings are anything but clear, strong, and constant!)

In *The Wheel of Rebirth* the Teacher puts it this way –

In the past man manifested his magical powers through ceremonial and religious rites, but now he expresses them through organisation and through scientific methods. The written word and pictured image are primarily the magical weapons of your age. Those who use these powers to cheat, deceive and manipulate the unwary in order to gain their personal ends and further their selfish activities, are every bit as dangerous black magicians in their way as the men who created evil forms to serve them in olden days. For such activities also create forms, and the greater the energy employed in the development of an idea, the greater the form that ensouls it becomes. Man is discovering once more how he can harness the elements to serve him, and those who deliberately use this knowledge to create destructive forces such as poison gas, death rays, high explosives and the like, did they but know it, are creating terrific elementals on the inner planes who will follow them vengefully life after life.

The Law remains unchanged for every age, but as man becomes increasingly powerful on the mental, creative plane, so do his responsibilities become more serious and the dire consequences proportionately greater if he uses those powers wrongly. Hence it behoves him to be careful; for he can encircle himself with guardians of light or with hosts of destructive beings generated by thoughts of hatred, jealousy and bitterness.[11]

That this is no chimera is shown by the following extract from a recent letter from a friend:

A religious group had sent out an invitation to a certain speaker to come and give a talk at one of their meetings. Later they discovered that in fact this man had an evil reputation. If they put him off under any pretext, it was likely to cause more trouble than if they allowed the talk to go forward. So they decided to choose five of their members to sit in the front row and just beam love to the speaker when he came on to the platform. When he rose to speak this is exactly what they did. The result was as follows: Within two minutes of starting his talk, he began to stammer. Within five minutes he had sat down. He was then escorted off the platform and that was the end of the matter.

The analogy of the iron filings and the magnetic field may also be helpful in relation to prayer. Suppose that on the laboratory bench are a powerful electro-magnet and a small magnet which can be moved about. Let us suppose that the electro-magnet represents a source of divine power, and that the small movable magnet signifies the personal self. The field due to the electro-magnet will be least distorted and the pattern of iron filings similarly so when the movable magnet occupies the same position as the electro-magnet, i.e. when the human will coincides with the Divine will. Moreover, the field will be at its strongest when the maximum permitted current flows through the electro-magnet (in response to prayer?), and our own magnetic field coincides with that of the electro-magnet. An interesting commentary on the idea of associating prayer with energy is provided by the following extract from *The Way of Companionship* by Margery Eyre –

> Again I take you into these inner worlds to show you more clearly the models from which you work on earth . . . Here within, form is not accentuated, for that is the later development in earth hands, but design is conceived, and great currents of power selected to carry it out, which must be mentally controlled throughout the whole process . . . There is also a dynamic centre to be created and attached to the design which is not wholly native to the inner planes but must partake also of earth vibrations. This is often the most difficult part of the work, for a sum of prayer must be found that is not already attached to an object and which can therefore be tapped and used . . . When the design and its dynamo have been successfully connected, attention has to be focussed and maintained to prevent disruption by the blindness of earth conditions.[12]

Comparable observations from a communicator 'on the other side' are given in *The Testimony of Light*[13] by Helen Greaves and *Collapse & Comeback*[14] by George Meek.

In the Gospels Jesus had this to say about prayer:

> Verily I say unto you, Whosoever shall say unto this mountain, Be thou taken up and cast into the sea; and shall not doubt in his heart, but shall believe that what he saith cometh to pass; he shall have it.[15]

> The works that I do shall he do also; and greater works than these shall he do.[16]

And as a condition of mighty works faith – 'the substance of things hoped for, the evidence of things not seen'[17] – is invariably stressed as all important. For example, 'According to your faith be it done unto you.'[18] To the writer to the Hebrews faith meant not an acceptance of a doctrine imposed by an authority outside himself, to whose wisdom he was ready to defer, but an intuition of his own soul that the things for which he hoped were real. In terms of the analogy of the iron filings and the magnetic field, is it not a straightforward case of cause and effect, namely that if the magnetic field (representing the etheric, which reflects thinking and feeling) is of sufficient strength, clarity, and constancy, then the reaction of the iron filings (representing the physical environment or the human body) is automatic and immediate? What is lacking is our faith that we can do it. And for this, extended physical sight, the ability to see the etheric would seem an almost essential prerequisite.

For some readers, the last few pages will doubtless seem very strange, but before what has been suggested is dismissed as fantasy it is worth reflecting on the nature of the physical world, the solids, liquids, and gases, which we take so much for granted. On an ultimate analysis these are immensely complex energy patterns in space that is other-wise empty. But this is a far cry from the table at which I am writing or the chair on which I am sitting. What is so remarkable – though not so regarded because it is happening all the time – is the capacity of the human mind to interpret energy patterns in space that is otherwise empty as tables and chairs, replete with secondary qualities such as colour, hardness, and smell. We fail to realise, or if we realise we overlook, the extent to which we live *here and now* in a thought created world.

So far this chapter has been concerned with the action of mind on matter, with the existence (at present hypothetical) of different grades of matter, and with the existence, function, and importance, of the health aura or etheric field. The most promising, if not essential, condition for progress in this area requires open-minded scientists and a trained clairvoyant working together. And by a trained clairvoyant is meant someone who has indeed been trained, either in this life or in some previous life or lives, and who can 'see', at will and as required, on the etheric, emotional, and mental levels. As already mentioned, such people are exceedingly rare, but they do exist. They seldom, if ever, come before the general public, because they regard their faculty as a sacred trust which is not to be used for other than spiritual purposes. They are not to be confused with the much larger number of people who claim to have occasional flashes of this or that, but who are rarely quite sure what it is they have 'seen'.

Other areas of the paranormal for which there is a steadily increasing body of evidence and which have far reaching implications and therefore merit investigation, cover telepathy, including telepathic communication with those who have died, out-of-the-body experiences, and experiences suggestive of reincarnation.

The main obstacle to investigating these fields is an innate and widespread psychological blockage to accepting the possibility that there is anything to investigate. The cause of this attitude is almost certainly the realisation, probably largely unconscious, of just how far reaching the results of such investigations could be. There is an underlying fear that a number of much cherished assumptions and presuppositions, both scientific and religious, will need to be jettisoned or at least undergo radical transformation.

That telepathy between the living can and does occur from time to time is now accepted by almost everyone, albeit reluctantly by many scientists. But very few are prepared to countenance the possibility of thought transference between someone who is living and someone who has died. Yet the evidence for this provided by, for example, *The Testimony of Light*[13] by Helen Greaves or *Gateway*[19] by Roger Whitby, is surely very strong. And if there are a few people, admittedly very few at present, who are capable of acting as telepathic communicators, is it not sensible to consider how such a faculty can be cultivated? At present very little seems to be being done with this in view. And would it not be only common sense to investigate the ideas and suggestions contained in a book such as *Telepathy and the Etheric Vehicle*[20] by Alice Bailey?

The evidence for 'out-of-the-body' experiences piles up and is now very large. But when considering the interpretation of these experiences, psychical researchers divide into two groups. One group thinks that the explanation resides in the existence of a very special ESP faculty; the other that out-of-the-body is literally the case, and that during an out-of-the-body experience consciousness does indeed function in some kind of vehicle *outside* the physical body. Having regard to the examples quoted in *The Sacred Quest*, the writer is a firm supporter of the latter of these two groups. This whole field is surely one where collaboration between open-minded scientists and a trained clairvoyant is vital.

Reincarnation, or serial existence, is a subject in which public interest has grown enormously over the past twenty-five years. In a poll undertaken for *The Sunday Telegraph* during 1981, the proportion of people who considered that there was something in the idea came out at 28%, an increase from 18% in a comparable poll ten years previously. But in scientific circles the concept and its implications are rarely mentioned, and in religious circles almost never. How very strange! How strange, too, that the collection and analysis of cases suggestive of reincarnation seem almost confined to Professor Ian Stevenson and his team at the University of Virginia. The use of hypnosis is, however, increasing – cf. *Life before Life* by Helen Wambach[21] and *Many Lifetimes* by Joan Grant and Denys Kelsey[22] – and it may be that this kind of evidence will eventually become compelling.

Astrology, too, may now merit a good hard look. Not the trivial entertainment which appears in a number of newspapers and weeklies, but the dozen or more page character sketch which is produced from date and place of birth and nothing else. After reading some of these character appraisals, it is difficult – in spite of a total absence of, at present, any rational explanation – to accept the blessed word 'coincidence' as an acceptable explanation of so many of the features correctly described in many horoscopes.

A fitting end to this chapter are some words of the Teacher in *The Wheel of Rebirth* –

> So small a part is perceptible on the physical plane of what a man is and of what he is striving to become. The modern psychotherapists realise this and are seeking to open to mankind the door of freedom through the power of the great occult formula *Man – know thyself*. But more is needed still; in the future, when the educationalists and healers have been able to develop their higher clairvoyance, and can perceive the true condition of their brothers in affliction, a great change will come over all the methods now used both with regard to the treatment of the sick, that of the insane and those with criminal tendencies. But it is essential for this development that the Law of Karma and reincarnation should be more generally accepted and studied than it is today. When it is taught, as it will one day be, from earliest childhood and taken into consideration in every circumstance of life, men will not continue to suffer blindly and to revolt against the apparent cruel compulsion of living in a universe governed either by blind Fate or a capricious god. [23]

References

1. *The Metal-Benders*, J. B. Hasted, (Routledge & Kegan Paul, 1981)
2. *Blueprint for Immortality*, H. S. Burr, (Neville Spearman, 1972)
3. *Subtle Body*, David Tansley, (Thames and Hudson, 1977)
4. *Radionics and the Subtle Anatomy of Man*, David Tansley, (Health Science Press, 1972)
5. *The Loom of Creation*, Dennis Milner & Edward Smart, (Neville Spearman, 1975)
6. *The Awakened Mind*, Maxwell Cade & Nona Coxhead, (Wildwood House, 1979)
7. *The Unseen Self*, Brian and Marita Snellgrove, (Kirlian Aura Diagnosis, 1979)
8. *Man Incarnate*, P. D. Bendit & Laurence Bendit, (Theosophical Publishing House, 1957), pp. 19 and 23
9. *The Psychic Sense*, P. D. Payne and L. J. Bendit, (Faber & Faber, 1958), p. 97

10. Same as ref. 8, p. 25
11. *The Wheel of Rebirth*, H. K. Challoner, (Rider & Co., 1935, republished by the Theosophical Publishing House, 1969), p. 111
12. *The Way of Companionship*, Margery Eyre, (Psychic Press, 1978), p. 135
13. *Testimony of Light*, Helen Greaves, (Published for The Churches' Fellowship for Psychical & Spiritual Studies by The World Fellowship Press, 1969, republished by Neville Spearman)
14. *Collapse and Comeback*, George W. Meek, (Metascience Corporation, U.S.A. 1979), p. 12
15. Mark 11:23
16. John 14:12
17. Hebrews 11:1
18. Matthew 9:29
19. *Gateway*, Roger Whitby, (Psychic Press, 1979)
20. *Telepathy and the Etheric Vehicle*, Alice A. Bailey, (Lucis Publishing Co., 1950)
21. *Life before Life*, Helen Wambach, (Bantum Books, 1979)
22. *Many Lifetimes*, Joan Grant and Denys Kelsey, (Corgi Books, 1976)
23. Same as ref. 11, p. 252

9: The Significance for Society

The significance of the spiritual vision in relation to the whole experience of man can be compared to the significance of the vision of 20th century science in relation to our understanding of the physical universe. Modern physics has uncovered dimensions of physical being of almost unimaginable size. In a strict sense these dimensions – the very large and the very small – are unimaginable since imagination is inevitably rooted in actual experience. When the physicist calculates that the age of the current physical universe may be about 3×10^{10} years, or that the laws of sub-atomic structure probably came into being between 10^{-40} and 10^{-20} seconds after the 'big bang' from which the universe may have originated, what we are really saying is that our abstract calculations about the nature of physical being reach far beyond the limited and partial experience provided by our five physical senses. But this involves a profound paradox. For abstract calculations which have taken modern science to the farthest boundaries of space and into the innermost recesses of the atom are all based in our commonsense world of human experience. The evidence is in the form of photographs and electronic instruments which we can see and touch, and the calculations and arguments are made by human beings like ourselves. That the unimaginably vast and unimaginably small intersect with the familiar here and now is, on reflection, strange and paradoxical.

In the perspective of modern physics, the world of commonsense experience is just a thin band within the entire spectrum of physical reality. Our eyes and ears only pick up a minute selection of the frequencies which are physically there. In the same way, the significance of the spiritual vision is that the whole physical universe from the tiniest packet of sub-atomic energy to the furthest galaxy of a billion suns is in turn nothing but a thin slice of a far greater reality. From this it follows that the spectrum of consciousness extends far beyond its highest visible manifestation among the peaks of human genius. In the words of the Teacher quoted in Chapter 6:

> There are many many planes of life. We may be on a plane some distance beyond yours, but there are planes beyond ours, far far beyond ours, of which we know very little. We know about as much of those planes as you know of ours. There are many planes, not one, hidden, as your Church tries to tell you.

The truth is that we do not know, and even the greatest mystic can only point. But such a spiritual perspective transforms the whole understanding of human knowledge and experience. In the light of the spiritual vision, philosophy, science, religion, the arts and politics, all become something different.

The arguments for the reality of the transforming spiritual vision have been given already, but can be summarised under three headings.

First, materialist 19th century physics, by pursuing its inquiries to their limits, has destroyed itself. For 20th century physics conceives multi-dimensional universes which are at least as strange as the quantum mechanical substructure of the atom. When contemplating the discoveries of modern science about the very large or the very small, the hard world of commonsense fades, space and time become something different, and the boundary between matter and consciousness becomes problematical.

Second, the paranormal and supernormal powers at the fringe of ordinary consciousness can no longer be ignored. For they exist. Telepathy and telekinesis tell us that the connection between matter and consciousness must be something quite other than that given in the standard materialist picture. No longer can self-consciousness be thought of as a peculiar anomaly, a 'ghost in the machine', trapped inside the bone box of the skull.

Third, the materialistic philosophies and psychologies of the 19th and 20th centuries have systematically turned their faces away from the peaks of human experience. It is not only the great mystics and religious teachers who have been raised in ecstatic vision to see that a unity of Spiritual Being pervades alike all human consciousness and the whole universe of space and time. Again and again this vision has also inspired the sublimest works of genius in poetry, music, philosophy, architecture and the arts generally. When men and women have reached upwards towards the highest and noblest picture of reality which they can conceive, this unity is what they have visioned. The cultural and dogmatic expressions of the religious impulse are confused, contradictory and sometimes may even be repulsive, but the drive towards a union with the Ground of Being, towards worship and spiritual enlightenment, and the drive towards self-transcendence are deeply rooted in human nature.

There is, moreover, a fourth consideration. It is an argument peculiar to, and appropriate to, our sceptical age with its agnosticism, its uncertainties, and its cynical view that all truth is relative. The 'official' materialist view of reality is that life and consciousness have evolved on this planet by chance: that the random operation of the physical laws of nature have produced complex chemical molecules which are capable first of life, and later of that sophisticated reflex of self-awareness which we call consciousness. The spiritual vision is the opposite hypothesis. It affirms that all that exists has come about through the operation of a divine spirit from which the entire universe has proceeded, and to which all that exists will one day return.

This spiritual conviction has found expression in the writings of many great souls. Wordsworth has given perhaps one of its finest expressions in his 'Tintern Abbey' –

. . . a sense sublime
Of something far more deeply interfused,
Whose dwelling is the light of setting suns,
And the round ocean and the living air,
And the blue sky, and in the mind of man:
A motion and a spirit that impels
All thinking things, all objects of all thought,
And rolls through all things.

From the cold perspective of 20th century knowledge we do not *know* that the spiritual vision is true. The occasional mystic possessed by his noetic vision may know, but he is a rarity. Even those whose lives have been transformed by some peak experience do not know for certain how, as in a jig-saw, the different pieces of human knowledge and experience fit together. But the 'official materialist' does not *know* either. The questioning agnosticism of our time which has destroyed many of the beliefs (as distinct from the foundations) of the older religious faiths, should also be applied to 'official materialism' which is based on assumptions that are clearly dated and demonstrably limited. We just do not know *how* matter and consciousness interact, and merely in terms of logical philosophy it seems systematically impossible to reduce consciousness to material terms. The spiritual vision therefore presents an alternative and wider hypothesis. There is no need to make a submission of faith. It is sufficient to take the spiritual vision as a provisional hypothesis, and then see what insights it gives into our condition.

From the perspective of the spiritual vision the 20th century is a time of near spiritual bankruptcy. That it should be so is, perhaps, inevitable. For over one and a half millenia the Christian religion – the teaching of Jesus *and the theological super-structure erected upon it* – provided a vision of spiritual meaning and purpose which has guided Western civilisation. The significance of spiritual experience and the justification of the self-transcending moral intuitions of compassion, humility and forgiveness, were all understood in a Christian context. But times have changed. During the last two centuries rational scholarship and the growth of scientific understanding have progressively undermined many previously held beliefs. Faced with the vastness of the physical universe as shown us by modern science, it is very hard to believe that the one, particular and unique incarnation of God took place on this tiny planet just under two thousand years ago and that no equivalent event has ever occurred anywhere else in the cosmos. And if we believe it, we are not believing what the early Church believed. Because for St Paul and his successors, the earth and the universe were more or less the same thing, since the universe was simply the earth with the sun, moon and stars, circling round it. Moreover, this cramped geocentric universe was confined in an equally cramped anthropocentric time scale. The chronology of the Bible dates the creation only 4004 years before the birth of Jesus, and some, at least, of the authors of the New Testament expected the world to end within their own lifetimes.

The dogmatic structure of Christianity was built up on the Pauline doctrine that Jesus Christ was the Saviour, whose atoning death on the Cross ransomed mankind from the penalties of sin and death that had been visited on them by God as a punishment for the disobedience of the first man, Adam. Taken literally such a doctrine is scientifically, morally and theologically unacceptable in terms of 20th century sensibility, and, of course, the number of Christians who do take it literally is, today, very small indeed. But, that said, what is the non-literal interpretation which takes the place of the literal one? The answers are multifarious and far from clear. Hence widespread confusion and disenchantment, and the questioning and experimenting, especially amongst the young, which characterise so much of the current scene.

For some considerable time Western civilisation has been spurred on by the drive for progress, with the confident expectation that as time passed and as a result of scientific discovery everything would get better and better. And over the years many things have indeed got better, much better. The advance of science from Galileo and Newton to Einstein and today's sub-atomic physicists has opened out vast new horizons for our understanding of the physical universe. And it is only necessary to think back to the squalor, ignorance, and expectation of life of the mediaeval peasant to realise how much his/her lot has improved, at least in many parts of the world. But material progress is two edged. Upwards of 40% of the world's scientific research and development is now being devoted to military purposes,[1] to inventing and developing 'better' weapons of destruction, the eventual outcome of which could be the end of human life, maybe all life, on this planet. Progress? Of a kind no doubt. But of a kind to be desired and encouraged?

The point, often overlooked, is that progress can be regarded from two quite different standpoints. From a spiritual standpoint progress implies increasing sensitivity to values such as beauty, truth, goodness and compassion. From a material standpoint, progress is a matter of means, means to an end, but is not an end in itself. And it is the ends which determine whether material progress is good or bad, desirable or undesirable. Until this century progress was regarded as almost automatic and essentially good. But World Wars I and II cast doubt on the validity of this assumption, and the recent development of the nuclear arms race has led to widespread disillusionment and loss of nerve. Over the future of material progress hangs a very large and menacing question mark.

The dynamic behind scientific progress has not been without influence on the rest of European civilisation – on religion, politics, and culture generally. Because of the rate at which one scientific hypothesis has outlived its usefulness and been replaced by another – a process to which Macneile Dixon refers in his Gifford Lectures[2] as 'science shedding its last year's conclusions as a snake its skin' – there has arisen the feeling that whatever is old and established has outlived its usefulness and is due to be replaced by something new. Such a feeling is the product of a very dangerous half truth. In science it is not the experimental facts, the data, which outlive their usefulness and are discarded – despite Einstein's theory of relativity, apples continue to fall to the ground! – but the conclusions and interpretations which they seem to justify. As the scope of the data increases, the conclusions and interpretations will alter. But in spite of being continuously added to, the data, qua data, remain unaltered. The half truth referred to above consists in the failure to recognise this fact and to cast out everything, the data as well as the conclusions which are drawn from it. In the case of religion such an attitude is disastrous. Because it means that the *foundations* – the sayings of World Teachers such as Guatama the Buddha, and Jesus the Christ – are considered as inapplicable and out of date as the theological super-structure erected by people who lacked the wisdom and insight of the original Teachers. In the contemporary scene there are many instances – and not just in religion – where the baby has been, or is being, thrown out with the bathwater.

If the history of a culture is depicted in its art, then the art of the 20th century is witness to our condition. When we consider, and try to come to terms with, the dominant characteristics of today's music, painting, literature and architecture, it will aid our understanding if we accept that their most fervent apologists and their severest critics are both correct. It is inevitable that the most sensitive and creative members of the community should act as forerunners of the age that is to be: that 20th century composers should have tried to go beyond the tonalities of Bach's equi-tempered clavier so as to explore new combinations of sound, and that visual artists living in an age of abstract science should have turned away from visual representation to explore new possibilities of shape and colour. The problem is that outside a limited circle of creators and 'with-it' critics, modern art and modern 'classical' music are not popular when compared with the art and music of previous centuries. The work of the modern artist or composer seems ugly, unharmonious and meaningless in comparison with that of earlier times. There is no depiction of grandeur, no apparent striving for beauty, no searching for spiritual meanings that evade verbal expression. Contemplation of 20th century art or music does not appear even to attempt the sublimity of the compositions of Bach or the paintings of Michelangelo. And it is disingenuous for the defenders of modern art to say that the modern artist is merely in advance of the popular taste, and that this has always been the case with creative artists. As a comment on previous ages, this is just not true. In the Renaissance, for instance, artistic innovation was applauded in the way that scientific advances are recognised now. So-called 'modern' art and music still only appeal to a sophisticated minority. Their defenders claim that this is due to their revolutionary newness. But they are as old as Einstein's Theory of Relativity and in the interval we have gone from the steam engine to the space rocket. Popular educated taste may be cruder, slower and less adventurous than that of the creative avant-garde, but it remains rooted in something which the avant-garde has deliberately rejected, the deep instinct for beauty, order and harmony. The more honest, or the more extreme, proponents of the avant-garde, have made it quite clear that they dislike and reject the traditional artistic canons of beauty and meaning. In a profound sense the 20th century has spawned the art of anti-art, and some of the most creative minds of our century have deliberately put the process of artistic creation into reverse. Cancer is a condition in which a group of cells kick over the traces irrespective of the needs and structure of the body as a whole. Unchecked the result is death. In a profound sense much of the art of the 20th century is cancerous.

If we suppose that the destiny of the human race is the upward path of spiritual enlightenment, the crisis of modern art is understandable and inevitable. For the 20th century stands in the interlude between the demise of the old pattern of spiritual vision offered by the dogmas of the Christian Church, and the emergence of a new and profounder spirituality. In this interlude 'God is dead', and human consciousness must seem but a brief flicker of self-consciousness in the random chaos of a meaningless universe. And this condition, this anguish, must be reflected in modern art.

In the spiritual vision the highest aspect of man is something which transcends intellect and emotion. This is the soul, the source of creativity and intuition and the point of synthesis for the energies, insights and powers of the intellect and the emotions. Without awareness of this central point of synthesis the personality tends to disintegrate and intellect and emotion become warring forces equally impoverished by the lack of the other. The art of the 20th century shows very clearly this disintegration: an abstract arid intellectualism pulling in one direction and a violent undisciplined emotionalism pulling in another. If, as Walter Pater said, all art aspires to the condition of music,[3] then nothing illustrates better the cultural crisis of the West in the 20th century than the typical musical compositions of our time – the unlistened to abstract academic compositions broadcast on BBC's Radio 3, and the direct, crude, emotional abandon of pop music and punk rock.

If this diagnosis is right, the progressive movement which has inspired Western culture has become corrupt because of the lack of inward spiritual vision. And this lack goes far to explain today's moral and political crisis in the Western World. A few years ago the Teacher referred to in Chapter 6 remarked:

> These are times of great decision, great threatening, and great disillusionment. The past order, the stability and the values which your generation took for granted, have now almost entirely collapsed as things to be taken for granted. The field of values can never be destroyed, but it has been eroded by the present agnosticism, doubt and cynicism. It is cynicism in high places that has destroyed the fabric of the life you knew.

There will be political difficulties amongst the young; these will increase rather than decrease. The reason for this is the failure of their teachers and elders; nothing constructive leading to the full flowering of the personality has been shown them. They have merely been taught with cynicism that everything that is established at the moment is by that fact wrong, but nothing durable, lasting, noble has been put in its place.

A root cause of this crisis is a misunderstanding of the nature of freedom. The West prides itself on being a free society, but the image of freedom we all too often possess is that of 'negative liberty', an image in which freedom is equated with lack of restraint. This is the freedom of modern art where the only rule is to find a rule and break it. It is the freedom of self-expression regardless of social consequence proclaimed by Existentialist philosophers. It is the freedom of permissiveness carried to its limit. It is the freedom of anarchy. But the freedom of anarchy is ultimately intolerable. I may wish to do what I like, but I find it insufferable when others do what they like regardless of me. As Thomas Hobbes observed,[4] life where all men are free to do as they like is so intolerable that men will gladly surrender their freedom to an absolute ruler in return for a guarantee of law and order. The progressive movement in morals and politics shows the same trend towards disintegration as modern art. Both in the end become intolerable.

A careful examination of various popular progressive causes indicates that many pass through a similar development cycle, or swing of the pendulum. What begins as a liberating protest against some restrictive tradition or oppressive social institution often becomes wilder and more extreme until the protest movement itself is as violent, or oppressive, or restrictive of human freedom as whatever sparked off the original protest. Thus the movement for greater honesty about human sexuality begins with a reaction against Victorian prudery and has ended with the mass media preoccupied with sexuality in greater public detail than has ever been known since the end of the Roman

147

Empire. The feminist movement starts as a protest to win equal respect for half the human race, but often seems to end with a dislike not only of men, but also of motherhood. Careful analysis of the movement against racism, and the campaign for nuclear disarmament, show the same tendency in operation. What starts off as generous and noble gradually becomes intolerant and destructive. Something which begins by desiring the good of society gradually becomes alienated from it.

The psychology of C. G. Jung provides a profound and provocative model of the nature of the human psyche. Freud saw human nature in terms of a frail crust of reason covering the bubbling volcanic instinctual drives for sex and destruction, and the behaviourists reduce the grandest aspirations of human consciousness to a mere inward reflection of basic animal behaviour reflexes. By contrast, Jungian psychology is optimistic. According to Jung man's dreams and intuitions point to a fuller and wiser psychic reality beyond the limits of immediate everyday rationality.

Jung pictured the psyche as a dynamic equilibrium of forces, and in *Man and his Symbols*[5] he represented this equilibrium in terms of a sphere. The upper part of the sphere's surface symbolises the conscious self, that is, the thoughts, emotions and memories which are within the area of our deliberate attention and control. The lower part of the sphere, floating as it were in darkness, represents the unconscious self. Within the lighted upper surface, out of the thoughts and purposes with which we deliberately and consciously identify, we each construct our persona. Thus the soldier wants to be brave, the judge stern and fair, the mother devoted and kind. In time they may actually become what they want to be and what society expects them to be. To a considerable degree, therefore, our personas, our outward personalities, are our own constructs. But in the dynamic interplay of psychic energy, action produces reaction. The positive persona in the conscious mind has its negative opposite in the unconscious. The stronger the persona the more powerful is the negative shadow, its opposite. So according to Jung each one of us contains within our unconscious the very desires which we reject or repress in our conscious selves. Psychological ill-health and mental breakdown ensue when this balance is upset, and the forces of the shadow erupt into consciousness. Very often the result is destructive when the wild and anarchic forces of the shadow overthrow the conventional rational restraints of the persona. However, this inversion does not always result in what is conventionally evil or destructive. Religious conversion or the reform of desperate criminals into upright citizens is often the sign of a compassionate and sensitive shadow overturning a hard and selfish persona.

Thus far the Jungian picture does not go much beyond the psychoanalytic theories of Freud. But Jung went further, and this led to the crucial differences which separated him from Freud. For Jung the aim of psychoanalysis is not merely to restore the balance between persona and shadow for those in whom this balance had become disturbed – the conventionally mentally ill. According to Jung, the aim of psychoanalysis is to go beyond both the conscious persona and the unconscious shadow to reach a point of synthesis. This point of synthesis Jung termed the 'soul'. In terms of the image of the sphere, the persona is the lighted upper surface, the shadow is the darkened under part, and the soul is the sphere's centre. In this image the soul, though below the threshold of consciousness, is totally different from the unconscious desires which make up the shadow.

According to Jung the aim of human life is to achieve integration, that is, bringing into a deliberate and self-aware unity all the conflicting forces which make up the persona and the shadow. For in that unity lies both wisdom and psychic strength. Achieving integration therefore depends upon attaining conscious awareness of the soul, the centre of the psychic being. Jung used the word 'soul' deliberately because he recognised that the techniques of religion, prayer, meditation, confession and participation in a meaningful liturgy, all

149

promoted the self-awareness which ultimately led to consciousness of the soul. Thus for Jung religion was psychologically true because, regardless of the intellectual coherence of its dogmas, the sincere belief and practice of a religion led to psychological integration. But towards the end of his life Jung did publicly express the view that not only was religion psychologically true, but that it was also ontologically true. In other words, that the discovery of the soul led on to the recognition of a real spiritual dimension beyond it. When asked if he believed in God, Jung replied 'I do not believe, I know'.

Not only may Jungian psychology give us insight into the psyche of each individual, it may also have something to say about the collective psychology of Western civilisation in the 20th century. In one of his books Jung wrote of *Modern Man in Search of a Soul*.[6] Although this book was written during the years between World Wars I and II, it is abundantly clear that the title is as apt today as it was then. The fact that there are in the world over fifty thousand nuclear warheads, sufficient to kill every man, woman and child on the planet many times over, and that 570 million people are severely undernourished at a time when the EEC does not know what to do with its food surpluses,[1] is proof enough of that. It is not only individual men and women but our whole civilisation which is at sea and without a compass. A thought provoking image is its quintessential product, the big city – a ring of prosperous outer suburbs, intersected by motorways and with jet planes overhead, but the inner city itself, decayed, deprived, and a synonym for social breakdown. We need the central balancing point of a meaningful religious tradition with wide reference points across our art and morals, our politics and science. We are lacking a central point of spiritual synthesis.

The spiritual vision reveals the crisis of Western civilisation in clear, if not lurid, relief.[7] But if the crisis of our time is spiritual bankruptcy, the path of spiritual enlightenment is the answer to that bankruptcy.[8] In the vision of man as a spiritual being, the demands of man's religious nature, the procedures of scientific enquiry, and the humanistic ideal of progress are all reconciled. The outlines of such a synthesis have been sketched already in this century by the Christian scientist and mystic Pierre Teilhard de Chardin,[9] and by the Hindu philosopher and mystic Sri Aurobindo.[10] Independently of each other both men seized the path of the evolution of consciousness as the hinge which joins the older religious traditions of the past with the dynamic scientific processes of the present. Both Teilhard and Aurobindo saw inward mystical experience as a higher potential of human consciousness to which all mankind should aspire, and both saw that the inner path of spiritual evolution linked man with a far vaster process of cosmic evolution.[11] cf. The observation of the teacher referred to in Chapter 6: 'The Earth is part of a far far larger scheme [than just the earth].'

In this upward evolutionary ascent, society and man's place in society play a vital part. Teilhard saw the next phase of evolution as a 'mega-synthesis' which would bring mankind into a closer conscious unity than that which exists at the moment. In his terms, the result would be a Christ consciousness, which would lead towards the 'Omega Point', THAT to which all ultimately returns. Though expressed in a different vocabulary, Sri Aurobindo's vision is similar.

What does this reference to a closer conscious unity mean?[12] An analogy is often drawn between the spiritual evolution of society and the spiritual evolution of the individual. Physical evolution dovetails into conscious evolution and then into spiritual evolution. In his *Phenomenon of Man* Teilhard sketched out a long evolutionary chain in which the twin forces of 'complexification' and 'unification' provide the motive force and direction for the upward thrust of evolution. In the beginning energy 'crystallised' into sub-atomic particles, which then 'centred themselves' into atoms. In turn atoms united to form molecules, molecules – proteins, and proteins – the giant DNA molecule; and so the frontier was passed between chemistry and life. Thus far Teilhard's picture of evolution mirrors the materialist picture of the origins of life. Where Teilhard's theory goes beyond science and enters the realms of philosophical speculation and religious prophecy is in his systematic extrapolation of the evolutionary process beyond physical evolution into conscious evolution and then into spiritual evolution.

According to Teilhard each evolutionary advance produces an explosion of new forms of life that evolve in all directions as advantage is taken of the new opportunities. But only one line of evolution becomes the 'verticil', the pointer to the next advance. Thus there are many chemical elements, but only carbon has the chemical properties which make the protein possible. There are many combinations of proteins, but only one DNA structure, and that is common to all forms of life from amoeba to man. There are many forms of living cells and many ways in which these assemble in multi-celled animals, but of all the different phyla only one has led to the organisation of nerve cells along a backbone and thence to the evolution of the brain. Of the many types of animal with a cranium only one has led to the evolution of a highly complex brain and the appearance of man with his self-reflexive consciousness. The process of evolution is a prodigal expansion of experiment and a ruthless selectivity of result. Many are called but few are chosen. When applied to the structure of society, the above approach implies that of many possible forms only one will be the 'verticil'.

Teilhard held that the future of evolution was not to be imagined in terms of the appearance of a new super-race of men with larger brains and more sensitive fingers. Physically we are the same as the Paleolithic Cro-Magnon cave painters. What has taken place since is not physical evolution but cultural evolution. The luxurious artifacts that fill our homes, the means of rapid transport and mass communication that unify the globe, all are human achievements consequent on thirty thousand years of society, five thousand years of civilisation and three hundred years of modern science and technology. Indeed, most of the inventions that have made the modern world – radio, television, motor-car, aeroplane, micro-chip computer, nuclear power and nuclear bombs – have come into being during the life-time of people still living. For Plato, Shakespeare and Siddhartha Gautama such things were not even dreams, yet they reached the heights of intuitive insight and creative imagination. This raises the question as to whether mankind needs any more physical power or luxurious artifacts than it already possesses? The problem is how to use wisely and share fairly what we have got already. To guarantee the present population of the planet the standard of living of Southern California, all that is needed is to use intelligently what we already know. Our problems are moral, not technological.

If we ask what political and moral ideas are available to guide us in facing the problems of the 21st century, an obvious answer is Marxism. Should anyone doubt the importance of ideas in changing the world, it is only necessary to look at recent history to see the answer. Marx remarked that hitherto philosophy had only sought to understand the world; the important thing was to change it. Marx's disciples have done as he wished, and today a large fraction of the world is under Marxist governments. The moral motive power behind Marxism is outrage at the sufferings of the despised and rejected poor in a rich society. That outrage is as justifiable today in terms of the disparity between the rich West and the Third World, as it ever was in terms of the protest against the poverty of the Victorian working class. But though Marxism starts with moral fervour it is a system of thought which denies morality all inner meaning. Marxism is systematic dialectical materialism. All human thought, morality and values, are held to be a product of economic circumstances, and economic forces proceed by a process of inevitable conflict. Marxism starts with outrage at the selfishness of the rich oppressor, but ends with a theory of human nature which regards the oppressor just as much a pawn of circumstances as the revolutionaries who will inevitably destroy him.

A *minor* criticism of Marxism is that it is a failed science. It failed to predict the Russian and Chinese revolutions, which did happen, and predicted British, American, and German revolutions, which did not. A *major* criticism of Marxism is that it has been put into practice with as much consistency as any ideology or religion has ever been, and the result has been massive, organised and deliberate suffering on a monumental scale. Stalin's purges, Pol Pot's extermination of the third of the Cambodian population that could read and write, and the full story of the Chinese 'cultural revolution' are among the most hideous pages of human history. If the world's future is Marxist, then that future is bleak. If the upward evolution of society points towards a higher spiritual awareness then the way does not lie through Marxism. To say this is not to preach hatred against Russians, or Chinese, or Cubans, for they are full partners in our common humanity. It is simply to say that the system of government under which they labour offers no way.

What then about those states and systems which are in self-conscious opposition to political Marxism, those states that often refer to themselves as the 'West', or the 'Free World'? What vision of man and society inspires those societies opposed to Marxism? The answer is an ominous blank. There was a time when Western civilisation might have been termed Christian. It was always rather a long road from the austere teachings of Jesus to the complexities of European civilisation, but when that civilisation was dominated by the Christian church it certainly claimed that title. The words of the New Testament articulate the only way most of us know by which to express our instinct for love, for self-sacrifice, and for God. But for many the old forms have lost their vitality, and European civilisation is now post-Christian.[13] In terms of contemporary science, psychology, and moral sensitivity, the Pauline claim that Jesus was the Second Adam come to reconcile us with God through his atoning death is not so much unbelievable as unintelligible. So there is a 'God shaped blank'[14] in Western consciousness.

In modern Western civilisation there is no one dominant ideology, political code, or religious system. The modern West is a free society which rejects the restraints of authoritarian dogma or an official world view. But this very freedom is rooted in assumptions, explicit or implicit, all of which are just as strongly held as the dogmas of authoritarian societies. The Western libertarian assumptions are based on the belief that everyone has the right to do what they like provided only that they do not prevent others from doing the same. The real world is not quite as libertarian as this ideal, but since World War II Europe and North America have approached this ideal to a remarkable degree.

This simple ideal of permissive liberty should not be despised. It was the precondition of the rise of modern science, for without the right to enquire where one pleased and come to whatever conclusions seemed correct science could never have begun (and did not in fact begin in societies that were not to some degree free). The ideal of laissez-faire free trade is the basis of capitalist economics. Although much can be said against capitalism, it is pre-eminently the system under which industrial processes have been pioneered and developed and which has lifted up starving peasants and tribesmen sunk in ignorance to the prospect of affluence for all. The same freedom gives the modern arts their licence to experiment in every direction and to break every traditional rule. Some of the results of this creative freedom may be uncomfortable,[15] but in a free society no one is forced to enjoy them if they do not want to. At the very least the explosion of energy which this freedom has released compels admiration.

So the 20th century stands between two opposed political systems. On the one hand there is the East European Marxist system which places the working class and the state above the claims of the individual and which emphasises order, responsibility, and collective progress. On the other hand there is the Western Liberal Democratic system with its values of individual rights, permissive freedom, and self-expression. To the West, the East represents totalitarian authority and the police state repressive of human rights and dignity. To the East, the West is selfish, degenerate, and corrupted by the pursuit of affluence. Both are almost certainly right.

That the ideas which underlie attitude and outlook determine action is manifestly true of individuals. But it is also true of a society and its culture. The triumph of Marxism, the triumph of Christianity, the power and perils of atomic energy, all exemplify the triumph of ideas. The present malaise of Western culture is precisely because we have no meaningful and compelling vision of man and his destiny. The coherence given by the old mediaeval Christian world view has been shattered by the vistas of biological evolution and the vastness of the cosmos.

The spiritual evolutionary view of society, in the manner of Teilhard and Aurobindo, points the way to a noble middle path between Eastern collectivism and Western individualism. The next development in the evolution of society must involve a coming together of individuals into a closer conscious unity, but this unity will not be one that can be imposed by external authority. One pointer to this is the unity of science – the unity of all scientists in the pursuit of truth. In a democracy consensus politics is another expression of the way in which the individual becomes part of a group and accepts a group pattern without surrendering inner integrity. Other pointers to this new unity are the development of sensitivity towards the experience of others through the arts, and the expression of responsibility and compassion through moral action. Perhaps, too, the paranormal dimension of telepathy indicates a higher type of unity, the full potential of which can only be guessed at.

The first rung on this evolutionary ladder is the ideal of social responsibility. We accept a duty to be concerned for others, not only for others as individuals, but for others as constituting the fabric of society upon which we all depend as individuals. The second rung is the moral ideal of unselfish love. We not merely accept a duty – something which is cool and rational – but we feel a deep, heartfelt, and maybe disturbing concern. The next rung is religious and spiritual. We love our neighbour as ourselves because we *are* our neighbour.[16] Historically this was the highest guiding principle of Western civilisation – loving our neighbour because we were commanded to do so by God's Son and because we are all children of one Father. This wisdom is eternal, but it may need rephrasing. And the necessary rephrasing may start with the recognition that this is not just an arbitrary scriptural doctrine but a real and practical experience.

The ideal of responsibility, concern, and unselfish love throws the problems of the 20th century into clear relief. The evolutionary ideal is a noble middle path which combines creativity and selection, freedom and order, exuberant energy and the search for perfection. With this in mind it is interesting to reflect on the attitude of the West towards sexual freedom. To be progressive is to be permissive, and to be permissive is to tolerate and even advocate every variety of sexual relationship with fewer and fewer restrictions. The result is increasingly unstable marriages and a rapidly rising number of children who have been deprived of the comfort and security of the care of two well adjusted adults within a stable family. Just as the DNA molecule appears to be the only structure which can effectively act as the basis of life on this planet, it could be that the stable two parent family is the only sound basis for full individual achievement and effective social progress. This is not only Christian teaching, but also Hindu and Confucian. Here, as in many other stages in evolution there may be only one 'verticil'. If this is the case, the foundations of society are crucially dependent on an awakened sense of responsibility and love within the individual, qualities which cannot be provided by legislation or externally applied moral pressure.

The ideal of the higher unity of the human race highlights

157

the problems of political democracy. The ideals of representative and participatory democracy do indeed point along the centre line between repressive totalitarianism and selfish anarchy. But a hard look at the realities of Western democracy today indicates that the democratic ideal has in some way gone cold. As the tide of Western imperialism has ebbed, few of the newly independent states have managed to maintain a viable democracy in any Western sense. Many of the West's cultural achievements have been embraced with enthusiasm, but representative government, an impartial civil service, politically neutral armed forces and the practice of mutual tolerance between all political factions, have not. Though every consideration of political prudence and cultural reality has forced the nations of Western Europe together, the EEC is, in practice, but a loose association of states having very little vision or intent of creating a genuine European community. In practice the participation of individuals in the political life of Western states is limited, sporadic, and ineffective, and large areas of life such as industry and commerce have hardly begun to grapple with the problems of individual participation in the wider structures in which they work. These issues are hard, practical and detailed. There is no evidence at the moment of any really profound drive to solve them. Yet the coming problems of the 21st century will force us to do so – or perish. The impending micro-chip revolution will completely alter the basis of industrial production and the whole pattern of leisure, employment, and education. It presages a change comparable with the industrial revolution, but over a much shorter time span. An authoritarian society *might* be able to cope with the rapidity of the necessary changes. A deeply concerned, responsible, and truly democratic society should certainly be able to do so; but a confused anarchic society, with no higher ideal than permissive liberty, will not.

References

1. *The War Games that Superpowers Play*, D.M.A. Leggett & C. M. Waterlow, (Centre for International Peacebuilding, 1985), Chap. 2
2. *The Human Situation*, W. Macneile Dixon, (Edward Arnold, 1937)
3. *The Renaissance*, Walter Pater
   'All art constantly aspires towards the condition of music.'
4. *Leviathan*, Thomas Hobbes, Chap. XVII
5. *Man and his Symbols*, C. G. Jung, (Aldus, 1964)
6. *Modern Man in Search of a Soul*, C. G. Jung, (Kegan Paul, Trench, & Trubner, 1933)
7. *The Aquarian Conspiracy*, Marilyn Ferguson, (Granada, 1982)
8. *Spiritual Man in a New Age*, Canon Peter Spink, (Darton, Longman, & Todd, 1980)
9. *The Future of Man*, Teilhard de Chardin, (Collins, 1964)
10. *The Life Divine*, Sri Aurobindo, (Sri Aurobindo Ashram, Pondicherry, 1970)
11. *Ponder on This*. A compilation from the writings of Alice Bailey & Djwhal Khul. (Lucis Press, 1971)
12. *The Awakening Earth*, Peter Russell, (Routledge & Kegan Paul, 1982)
13. *Taking Leave of God*, Don Cupitt, (S.C.M., 1980)
14. *Campaigns for the Conversion of England*, issued by Press and Publication, Church Assembly, Westminster, 1946. (Report of a committee chaired by the Bishop of Warrington)
15. *Civilisation*, Kenneth Clark, (B.B.C. Publication, 1969)
16. *Eastern Religion and Western Thought*, S. Radhakrishnan, (O.U.P. 1939), p. 101
   At the end of his Indian tour, Dr Paul Deussen said to a gathering in Bombay: 'The Gospels quite correctly establish as the highest law of morality, "Love your neighbour as yourselves." But why should I do so since by the order of nature I feel pain and pleasure only in myself, not in my neighbour? The answer is not in the Bible . . . but is in the Veda, in the great formula "THAT ART THOU", which gives in three words the combined sum of metaphysics and

morals. You shall love your neighbour as yourselves because you are your neighbour.' In the words of the *Bhagavad Gita*: 'He who knows himself in everything and everything in himself will not injure himself by himself.' Every person round me is myself at a different point of space and time and at a different grade of being.

10: Summary and Conclusions

That our world is in deep trouble and beset with far reaching problems is obvious to all. Equally obvious is that such efforts as are being made to overcome these problems are not commensurate with what is needed. A particularly comprehensive analysis of our present predicament is contained in *The Seventh Enemy* by Ronald Higgins.[1] After spelling out the current confusion of attitude and outlook, he refers to six major threats any one of which could lead to disaster: too many people, too little food, shortage of resources, degradation of the environment, misuse of nuclear energy, and the ruthless exploitation of science and technology. All six threats have been the subject of innumerable reports, speeches, and conferences, both national and international. But with what result? The increase of world population continues unabated, scarce resources continue to be squandered, degradation of the environment goes on apace, and similarly for the other three threats. Indeed, the nuclear threat is now such that to continue the international arms trade and to proceed with the development of nuclear weapons is nothing short of madness. A recent article in the *British Medical Journal* titled 'The final epidemic' opens with this paragraph –

Just before Easter doctors from 30 countries met at Cambridge for the second congress of International Physicians for the Prevention of Nuclear War. Its main conclusions were chilling. Nuclear war is becoming more likely every year and any nuclear war is likely to be global; the medical services cannot possibly cope with the casualties either short term or long term. These doctors have become convinced that any detailed, practical,

161

realistic assessment of the outcome of a nuclear conflict shows that its consequences will be far worse than most people seem to realise. Not only will casualties be on a far larger scale than can easily be comprehended, but the explosion of thousands of large nuclear weapons seems very likely to cause such damage to the atmosphere, to agriculture and food production, and to ecological systems that the planet may become uninhabitable in biological terms.

In the face of all these threats to the future of human life, how is it that so little has been achieved? According to Higgins the answer lies in 'Political Inertia' and 'Individual Blindness' which together constitute what he refers to as 'The Seventh Enemy'. Expressed in different words, the seventh enemy is the combination of an inflexible attitude of mind – what the psychologists call 'perpetual set' – and lack of vision.

When motivation is strong, action follows. An observation which is as true for groups as it is for individuals. So what is lacking in the present context is sufficiently strong motivation. And what produces motivation? Answer – an aim, goal, or purpose to which the individual or group is totally committed. In a word, for matters such as those being discussed, a faith – which may be either secular or religious.

In this country the two most important faiths are Scientific Humanism and Christianity. Scientific Humanism, which assumes that the world of the five physical senses is all there is and so is devoid of religious content, represents in practice if not in theory the attitude and outlook of most people. Of those having a religious faith Christians are by far the most numerous, though there are sizable minorities of Jews and now of Moslems. But to an increasing extent since the end of World War I, the commitment of many adherents both of Scientific Humanism and of Christianity has become markedly less than total. And the underlying reason is the same for both. The absence of a statement of the meaning and purpose of human life on this planet which is comprehensive and convincing.

For the Scientific Humanist the material world is all there is. So that for everyone physical death is the end of the story. Logically this leads to a philosophy of 'let us eat, drink, and be merry for tomorrow we die'. And for many, this, tempered by varying degrees of kindness, is indeed their philosophy of life. Up to the outbreak of World War II, and to a lesser extent World War I, the Scientific Humanist believed that an ever increasing material standard of living would of itself bring in the millenium. Such an expectation is no longer tenable, and the growing realisation of this fact has led to widespread disillusion. In *Civilization on Trial* Arnold Toynbee has this to say –

> We have obviously, for a number of generations past, been living on spiritual capital. I mean clinging to Christian practice without possessing the Christian belief – and practice unsupported by belief is a wasting asset, as we have suddenly discovered to our dismay in this generation.[2]

For the Christian the world of the five physical senses is far from being all there is. But teaching about what exists outside it is vague to say the least, and when it comes to evidence so much is anchored to authority and based on events of long ago. This is found by increasing numbers to be unsatisfactory. More, a lot more, is now being looked for – in particular, cogent answers to the three fundamental questions posed at the end of Chapter 2. And the answers, to be acceptable, must be based on experience and experiment.

In neither Scientific Humanism, nor in Christianity as normally presented, is there a compelling and realistic vision of the future. *And this today is what is lacking.* There is a void which is sensed by many and by young people especially. A forthright and challenging appraisal of our condition is contained in the following extract from *A Treatise on White Magic.* ('White magic', in the words of Tudor Pole, 'is simply the operation of spiritual law in human affairs, unobstructed by man-made ignorances and

163

frictions. Because we know so little about the working of the Law, when we see a demonstration of its operation we call it magic; whereas it is spiritually natural, and will ultimately become universal.')[3]

Out of the darkness of time there have emerged the great religions . . . When men succeed in isolating that inner significant structure of truth which is the same in all climes and in all races, then there will emerge the universal religion. Theologies will disappear into the knowledge of God; doctrines and dogmas will no longer be regarded as necessary, for faith will be based on experience; and authority will give place to personal appreciation of Reality. The power of the Church over the group will be supplanted by the power of the awakened soul in men; the age of miracles, and the disputations as to the why and how of those miracles with the consequent scepticism or agnosticism, will give way to the understanding of the laws of nature which control the superhuman realm and the super-natural stage of the evolutionary process. Man will enter into his divine heritage and know himself as the Son of the Father, with all the divine characteristics, powers and capacities which are his because of his divine endowment. But in the meantime what have we? A breaking away from old established tradition, a revolt from authority. Hence we are passing through an intermediate stage of chaos and of questioning, of rebellion and consequent apparent licence. But out of the medley of ideas, theories, speculations, religions, churches, cults, sects and organisations, two main lines of thought are emerging – one doomed eventually to die out, the other to strengthen and grow.

These two lines are –

1. Those who look back to the past, who hang on to the old ways, the ancient theologies. These are the people who recognise authority, whether that of a prophet, a bible or a theology. These are those who prefer obedience to imposed authority to the self-imposed guidance of an enlightened soul.

2. The second group is as yet a very small minority, but a steadily growing one. It is that inner group of lovers of God, the intellectual mystics, the knowers of reality who belong to no one religion or organisation, but who regard themselves as

members of the Church universal and as 'members one of another'.

Connected with these two groups, the reactionary doctrinaires and the subjective band of mystics, is the majority of the new generation of young people who are part of neither band and whose ideas are largely disorganised by the recognition of both. This majority do not belong to the past and refuse to accept the authority of the past. They do not belong to the inner group of knowers, for they have not reached as yet the point of knowledge. They only recognise two things: their need for freedom, and an intense eagerness for knowledge.[4]

This passage, which was written with prophetic insight nearly fifty years ago, brings us back to further consideration of 'the seventh enemy' – the combination of an inflexible attitude of mind and lack of vision – and how it can be overcome. The change required in attitude of mind is from one which is bounded by authority and is unwilling to examine fundamental assumptions and presuppositions, to one that is open and founded on personal experience.

Science should be, and is for the most part, an open system. Indeed, this is one of its outstanding characteristics and the foundation of its success. When some hypothesis or theory does not work, it is discarded – throughout the world, too, not just in one country or nation. But there are areas on the borders of science where openness is lacking, and the paranormal is one of them. The reason is not far to seek. 'Orthodox science cannot incorporate psychic forces in the way it incorporated, say, magnetism, because psychic forces require not an adjustment, but an upheaval.' And in the same article in the *Radio Times* there is this revealing observation:

The want, or need, to *dis*believe can be so powerful as to override all other considerations.

There has been a typical example of this recently, which has led to the exposure of the American Committee for the Scientific Investigation of Claims for the Paranormal (CSICOP). Set up ostensibly to *be* scientific in its approach – unlike the

American SPR, the implication was – it began by investigating the 'Mars effect' discovered by Michel Gauquelin, which has suggested there must be something to astrology, after all. When the CSICOP trial confirmed Gauquelin's findings, it was suppressed – a fact which has only recently been made public by a dissident member of the Committee.[5]

Such an occurrence illustrates the importance of what was referred to earlier as 'perpetual set', and of the observation made by Arthur Koestler that

> To unlearn is more difficult than to learn; and it seems that the task of breaking up rigid cognitive structures and reassembling them into a new synthesis cannot, as a rule, be performed in the full daylight of the conscious, rational mind. It can only be done by reverting to those more fluid, less committed and specialised forms of ideation which normally operate in the twilight below the level of focal awareness.[6]

In Chapter 2, an examination of the Science and Religion controversy, reawakened by the publication of Darwin's *Origin of Species*, showed that much of the conflict was due to *each* party to the dispute making claims to which it was not entitled. In their attitude to the paranormal it behoves scientists not to repeat their mistake and to make destructive and unwarranted pronouncements on matters which lie outside the domain of science.

Religion, by contrast, is not for the most part an open system. The followers of a particular religion, especially the monotheistic religions, have tended to be intolerant and exclusive, as exemplified by the wars of religion and the appalling atrocities to which they gave rise. They have also shown a strong tendency to look back to the past rather than forward to the future. But today, as a consequence of increased mobility worldwide, and the pluralistic societies to which this leads, there are signs of change. In a letter received by the author in 1970, two Christian missionaries who had spent many years in India, said –

> An equally difficult conversion asked of us Christians is the acceptance of religious pluralism of diversity as God's gift, as

166

blessing, rather than as a challenge to renew any missionary crusade. The legacy of missions hangs very heavily around our necks and it is still hard for most Christians to say with Robert Antoine that 'the other religions are not fortresses which we must attack and destroy. They are homes of the Spirit which we have chosen to ignore.'

And in relation to Christianity Canon Peter Spink writes as follows –

> What then is the function of the religious system in relation to man's search for knowledge of the Truth? The Christian Scriptures and the ecclesiastical system pertain not primarily to knowledge, but to faith, and a clear distinction must be made between the two if we are to understand the nature of today's search. What is this distinction? Through their verbal transmission (i.e sacred books and community structures) religious bodies provide frameworks of faith. These frameworks are constructed through doctrinal definitions and established on dogmatic assertions. Within these frameworks the truth may be pursued but they do not themselves constitute Truth, and when defined in this way they relate to man's cerebral capacity to acquire and accumulate information. Truth in relation to the knowledge of the heart may be defined as that which in a given situation awakens to ultimate reality, no more and no less. It can never be identified with static form or a doctrinal definition. Though a verbal crystallisation may articulate and confirm the experience of reality, it cannot exist as an intellectual proposition appropriate to all situations nor can it be propagated as such. To identify the verbal transmission with that which awakens to reality leads only to confusion, for it merely increases the supply of information and reshapes processes of thought.[7]

Considering as an analogy a country and a map of that country, a 'framework of faith' corresponds to a map, while 'truth in relation to the knowledge of the heart' corresponds to the experience of actual exploration. Maps, as we all know, are of many different kinds, ranging from the accurate to the faulty, from the clear to the confusing. A good map can be invaluable, indeed, is almost a necessity when exploring unknown territory, but a bad one can invite disaster. Hence the great importance of ensuring that whatever map is used is a sound one.

The second requirement is the need for vision, and this is what *A Forgotten Truth* is essentially about: a vision that will give purpose and meaning to human life. As a matter of observation, consciousness and form are complementary aspects of everything that lives, and when considering vision something analogous holds good. There is consciousness per se; and the form in which that consciousness is enshrined. The former is the heart of religion and, as Peter Spink points out, cannot be verbalised; the latter is the metaphysic in which it is expressed. The metaphysic suggested in this book is portrayed by the allegories developed in Chapter 4, and the picture which emerges has something in common with the spiritual philosophy of Teilhard de Chardin as expounded in *The Future of Man.*[8]

The vital concept is that of spiritual evolution – the development over many lives of a consciousness which will enable us to perform whatever part we may be called upon to play in the drama of life with grace, skill, and selfless dedication. (For each and every member of the human family such an ability must apply, of course, to many parts, not just to one.) The method of achieving this state of consciousness is by trial and error and the overcoming of our failings through the experiences provided by serial exist-ence. Once the four cryptic statements on page 120 are understood and accepted – by the heart as well as by the head – then human life on this planet has indeed a compelling and long term purpose. An obvious but very important implication is in relation to responsibility. So long as it is thought that when we die we leave the planet and do not return, the motivation for dealing with the threats to the human family enumerated at the beginning of the chapter is muted. But when it is realised that what we create we shall individually and collectively inherit – and that there is no alternative – the situation undergoes a profound change, and so do human attitudes. No longer will there be any point in an individual or nation using unworthy means to get the better of another individual or nation.

Harking back to one of the allegories developed in Chapter 4 – that of life at school as an allegory of human life – there is at this time one particular question which comes to mind and which merits very serious reflection – 'What happens to the school if the children burn it down?'

We shall conclude with two quotations, the first by Kenneth Clark, the second by one of the Teachers referred to in Chapter 6.

> I believe that order is better than chaos, creation better than destruction. I prefer gentleness to violence, forgiveness to vendetta. On the whole I think that knowledge is preferable to ignorance, and I am sure that human sympathy is more valuable than ideology . . . I believe in courtesy, the ritual by which we avoid hurting other people's feelings by satisfying our own egos. And I think we should remember that we are a part of a great whole, which for convenience we call nature. All living things are our brothers and sisters.[9]

> The simplification of the attitudes of men and women is the crying need at this time. Ideologies must go; old ideals must be relinquished; petty political, religious and social schemes must be discarded, and the one driving purpose and the one outstanding determination must be the release of humanity from the imposition of fear, from enforced slavery and the reinstatement of men in freedom with due opportunity to express themselves through right human relations.

Epilogue

'Where there is no vision the people perish.'[10]

References

1. *The Seventh Enemy*, Ronald Higgins, (Hodder & Stoughton, 1978)

169

2. *Civilization on Trial*, Arnold J. Toynbee, (Oxford University Press, 1948), p. 237
3. *A Man Seen Afar*, W. Tudor Pole and Rosamond Lehmann, (Neville Spearman, 1965), p. 63
4. *A Treatise on White Magic*, Alice A. Bailey, (Lucis Publishing Co., 1934), pp. 326–330, in 5th edition
5. Article in the *Radio Times* for 13/19 February 1982
6. Quoted in *Intelligence Came First*, edited by E. Lester Smith, (The Theosophical Publishing House, 1975), p. 155
7. *The Nature of Truth*, Canon Peter Spink. Article in the *Burrswood Herald*, Easter 1980
8. *The Future of Man*, Teilhard de Chardin, (Collins, 1964)
9. *Civilization*, Kenneth Clark, (B.B.C. & John Murray, 1969), p. 346
10. Proverbs 29:18

Bibliography

Sri Aurobindo, *Essays on the Gita*, Aurobindo Library, 1950

Paul Beard, *Living On*, George Allen & Unwin, 1980

Alice A. Bailey, *From Intellect to Intuition*, Lucis Press, 1932

Fritjof Capra, *The Tao of Physics*, Wildwood, 1975

H. K. Challoner, *The Wheel of Rebirth*, Rider, 1935

Helen Greaves, *Testimony of Light*, Churches' Fellowship for Psychical & Spiritual Studies, 1969

The Wheel of Eternity, Neville Spearman, 1974

F. C. Happold, *Religious Faith & Twentieth Century Man*, Penguin, 1966

J. Head & S. Cranston, *Reincarnation in World Thought*, Julian Press, New York, 1967

David Hey, *Exploring Inner Space*, Penguin, 1982

J. Hick, *Death and Eternal Life*, Collins, 1976

Raynor Johnson, *The Imprisoned Splendour*, Hodder & Stoughton, 1953

A Pool of Reflections, Hodder & Stoughton, 1975

W. Johnston, *Silent Music*, Collins, 1974

The Inner Eye of Love, Collins, 1978

C. G. Jung, *Man and his Symbols*, Aldus, 1964

D. M. A. Leggett, *The Sacred Quest*, James Clarke, 1986

Lawrence LeShan, *The Medium, the Mystic & the Physicist*, Turnstone Press, 1974

David Lorimer, *Survival*, Routledge & Kegan Paul, 1984

S. Radhakrishnan, *An Idealist View of Life*, George Allen & Unwin, 1932

Peter Russell, *The Awakening Earth*, Routledge & Kegan Paul, 1982

Mark Satin, *New Age Politics*, Delta Books, 1979

Rupert Sheldrake, *A New Science of Life*, Blond & Briggs, 1981

Pitirim Sorokin, *The Ways and Power of Love*, Beacon, 1954

Peter Spink, *Spiritual Man in a New Age*, Darton, Longman, & Todd, 1980

W. T. Stace, *Mysticism & Philosophy*, Macmillan, 1961

Michael Talbot, *Mysticism & the New Physics*, Routledge & Kegan Paul, 1981

R. Targ & H. Puthoff, *Mindreach*, Paladin, 1978

Charles Tart, *Altered States of Consciousness*, Wiley, 1969

P. Teilhard de Chardin, *The Phenomenon of Man*, Collins, 1959

Lyall Watson, *Supernature*, Doubleday, 1973

Index